THE PARZIVAL MYSTERY STREAM IN THE TWENTIETH CENTURY

THE PARZIVAL MYSTERY STREAM IN THE TWENTIETH CENTURY

RICK SPAULDING

WRIGHTWOOD PRESS

ANN ARBOR

Copyright © 2023 by Rick Spaulding
All rights reserved.

Wrightwood Press
www.wrightwoodpress.org

Edited by Maurice York.
Book design and cover art by Maurice York.

The photographs on the facing page to the quote from Dr. King are: "Martin Luther King Jr. addresses a crowd from the steps of the Lincoln Memorial, USMC-09611," taken on 28 August 1963, a public domain photo retrieved from Wikimedia Commons; and "Civil Rights March on Washington, D.C (Marchers at the Lincoln Memorial)" taken 28 August 1963, held by the National Archives and Records Administration (NARA) under NAID 542053; this is a public domain photo also retrieved from Wikimedia Commons

NON-PROFITS, LIBRARIES, EDUCATIONAL INSTITUTIONS, WORKSHOP SPONSORS, STUDY GROUPS, ETC.
Special discounts and bulk purchases are available.
Please email sales@wrightwoodpress.org for more information.

April 2023
ISBN 978-0-9801190-8-4

To Walter "Slim" Coleman—a true community organizer and minister, a trusted advisor to Fred Hampton and Harold Washington, and a profound student of current events, which he is able to read in the light of Scripture and deliver their deeper meaning in the form of sermons.

Reverend Martin Luther King, Jr. and the assembled crowd at the March on Washington, August 28, 1963. The top picture looks out over the Reflecting Pool to the Washington Monument beyond; the bottom picture looks the opposite direction, back at the Lincoln Memorial and the steps from which Dr. King delivered his famous "I Have a Dream" speech.

And when we allow freedom to ring,
when we let it ring from every village and every hamlet, from every state and every city, we will be able to speed up that day when all of God's children, black men and white men, Jews and Gentiles, Protestants and Catholics, will be able to join hands and sing in the words of the old Negro spiritual:
Free at last. Free at last.
Thank God almighty, we are free at last.

—Dr. Martin Luther King, Jr
August 28, 1963

LIST OF CHARTS

Chart A:	The Circle of the Twelve Characters in *The Guardian of the Threshold*	14
Chart B:	The Possible Past Lives of Rudolf Steiner	18
Chart C:	The Three Tones (or Houses) in Shakespeare's *Hamlet*	34
Chart D:	The Circle of Twelve American Civil War Leaders and Their Three Tones	42
Chart E:	The Circle of the Great Heroes of Ancient Greece and Their Three Tones	58
Chart F:	The Circle of the Founders of the Roman Empire and Their Three Tones	59
Chart G:	The Circle of the Founding Fathers of the American Republic and Their Three Tones	64
Chart H:	The Columbian Legend (1788—1826)	72-73
Chart I:	The Possible Past Lives of Mahatma Gandhi	89
Chart J:	The Grail Mystery Stream Aiding Rudolf Steiner	104
Chart K:	A Possible Past Life of Martin Luther King, Jr.	117
Chart L:	A Comparison of the Three Pillars of the Social Movements for Nonviolence and Truth in the Twentieth Century	149
Chart M:	A Timeline of Nonviolent Social Movements in the Twentieth Century	152
Chart N:	A Possible Past Life of Malcolm X (El-Hajj Malik El-Shabazz) and of Huey Newton	175
Chart O:	The Grail Circle of Civil Rights and Human Rights Activists in America (1954—1987)	218
Chart P:	The Three Pillars of the Mystery Stream of Parzival in Twentieth Century America and the Three Groups of Elements that Contain their Co-Workers	219
Chart Q:	The Civil Rights and Human Rights Movements in America (1954—1987)	220

CONTENTS

1.	Rudolf Steiner's Research on Reincarnation	3
2.	Abraham Lincoln and the Civil War	30
3.	George Washington and the Legend of Columbia	55
4.	Mahatma Gandhi and the Independence of India	75
5.	Reverend Martin Luther King, Jr. and the Civil Rights Movement	105
6.	Nelson Mandela and the Anti-apartheid Movement in South Africa	132
7.	El-Hajj Malik El-Shabazz (Malcolm X) and the Black Power Movement	153
8.	Fred Hampton and the Rainbow Coalition	177
9.	Walter "Slim" Coleman and the Social Movement of Faith and Family Inspired by the Lady of Guadalupe in Twenty-first Century America	221

1.
Rudolf Steiner's Research on Reincarnation

In 1979, at the age of thirty-three, I joined the Anthroposophical Society and became a member of the Rudolf Steiner Group in Chicago. The following year, Dr. Traute Page, the president of the Chicago Group, offered to lead a study group on Steiner's *Mystery Dramas* (CW 14). I earned a living as an English teacher in the Chicago Public School system, and I looked forward to studying Steiner's plays. At the time, Saul Bellow had been studying Steiner's path of initiation privately with another leader of the Rudolf Steiner Group, Peter Demay. Though he came to one of the meetings of the Mystery Drama group, he did not participate in the discussions. His fame for winning the Nobel prize for literature in 1976, it was hoped, would attract media attention to the Anthroposophical Society and bring an increase in membership.

Steiner's dramas were a significant attempt to bring into the modern age what the tragedies of Aeschylus, Sophocles, and Euripides had brought to the age of ancient Greece. The Greek tragedies were part of the spring festival held at the Theatre of Dionysius. All Athenian citizens were required to attend, and some fifteen thousand people watched five trilogies performed over a five-day period. The seats of honor in the front row on either side of the central aisle were granted to the leader of the Dionysian mysteries and to Socrates. Each year five dramatists were chosen to have their plays put on stage, and one was selected as the winner. Sophocles and Euripides each won the prize twenty times.

The spring festival allowed the citizens of Athens to participate in the lesser mysteries, which were known as the fire trial and the water trial. The Greek religion took this particular form so that all citizens could experience the mysteries artistically. Only specially selected Athenians—the *mystae*—could participate in the greater mysteries, which took place in the fall in the city of Eleusis, west of Athens. On the pain of death, those secrets of initiation were not to be revealed to the uninitiated. Aeschylus, accused of revealing one of the greater mysteries in his plays, almost had to pay that penalty, but the leading initiate of the Eleusian mysteries testified at his trial and exonerated him. During this annual springtime celebration, the Athenians experienced the trials of Helen, Orestes, Medea, Ajax, Hecuba, and other famous heroes. Even today the few remaining tragedies wield remarkable power over their readers, as any who teach them can surely affirm. When these performances were given in the amphitheater of Dionysius—where sculptures decorated its precincts, actors wore painted masks, and dancers spoke in choruses—the glory that was Greece was at its height. The end of the creative output of the Greek tragedians signaled the close of the golden age of Greek culture.

Through the Mystery Dramas, Steiner sought to bring the modern form of the trials of initiation to the stage, which required him to take on the roles of playwright, director, set designer, and costume designer. Even more, he ushered in two new art forms—eurythmy and speech formation—all while working with volunteers and a non-professional cast of actors. Producing a new play each summer from 1910 to 1913, Steiner brought the fire trial and water trial—only hinted at in works like Mozart's "The Magic Flute"—to the light of day. Each of his four plays focuses on a different main character, whose trials become the center of the narrative action. To help the study group devoted to the Mystery Dramas in the fall of 1980, Dr. Page encouraged us to read each play with an open mind, letting it pour over us "as if just taking a shower." She warned against trying to fit the events into a schema and the temptation to intellectualize the meaning of the plays.

Throughout the *Mystery Dramas*, twelve individuals are working to accomplish a certain higher goal or mission, with some pursuing it actively and others becoming obstacles to its attainment. The group of twelve characters appear together in the final scene of the first play, *The Portal of Initiation*, and again in each of the other three plays. This concept of a twelve-fold group of people, repeatedly found in tropes such as the twelve tribes of Israel, the twelve disciples of Christ, and the twelve knights of the Round Table, could seem like an historical or literary device. Yet Steiner's dramas suggest that being in such a grouping is not only common but significant and bound up with the human condition itself.

For Steiner, creations of culture were incompatible with the onset of World War I, so the guns of August in 1914 stopped his pen from writing a fifth mystery drama. Instead he turned to another task—building a home for the mystery dramas, a modern temple of the spirit, the Goetheanum. This unique and magnificent building also became home to meetings of the Anthroposophical society, founded by Steiner in 1912. At the annual general meeting in 1914, he delivered a lecture cycle in which he further elaborated the concept of reincarnation as a regular progression through the twelve signs of the zodiac. As illuminated in the lectures on *Human and Cosmic Thought* (CW 151), reincarnation involves very specific clockwise movements of the individual through twelve successive worldviews—each a new incarnation—so that the intentions of specific hierarchical beings can shine through human thoughts and actions into the physical world: "Human beings are the thoughts of the gods." Exceptions to the prescribed movements do occur, but the fundamental lawfulness of moving gradually through the twelve worldviews in successive lifetimes allows each individual human ego to experience the world and its events more fully and completely.[1]

In these lectures, Steiner also developed the idea of the world-soul-moods as a further way of understanding the patterns and laws that guide human incarnation. He examined the seven world-soul-moods and explained how each can appear within a given worldview. He further explained how a human lifetime is characterized by the unfolding of one particular world-soul-mood within the particular worldview through

---

1 The zodiacal sign of one's worldview is generally different from that of one's so-called birth sign.

which the ego sojourns during its earthly life. Steiner drew on the language of Ptolemaic astronomy to compare the seven world-soul-moods to the seven planets, and the twelve world-views to the twelve signs of the zodiac. In Ptolemaic astronomy, the circular movement of each planet describes an arc, or sphere, while the constellations of the zodiac are fixed in place and arranged at regular intervals in a great circle, similar to the markings of a clock face. He described the cosmic mechanics of reincarnation as a vertical movement of the ego to the next higher planetary sphere accompanied by a clockwise shift to the next zodiacal sign in the following incarnation. The framework for understanding Steiner's idea of the complete cycle of reincarnation is called in astronomy the Platonic year, since Plato himself taught these ideas to his students at the Academy. Over the portal through which a student entered the Academy were the words, "Let none but geometricians enter here."

Among Steiner's many achievements was the creation of the pedagogical principles of the first Waldorf School. As with many of Steiner's initiatives, the key principles and foundational ideas of Waldorf education are captured in his lectures, which are studied to this day by teachers who attempt to bring these principles to life in thousands of Waldorf schools around the world. Waldorf elementary school teachers generally study Steiner's lecture cycle on the four temperaments and discover how helpful these ideas about the four types of life bodies (or etheric bodies) can be in practical classroom tasks, such as making out seating charts, helping instruct individual students, or disciplining students who misbehave. Some teachers even try to share this knowledge with parents who ask for assistance with rearing their child. Waldorf high school teachers are very much in the same situation as teachers of the first eight grades, though they are immersed in a later phase of child development. They stand in need of insight into the soul (or astral body) that manifests in the child around the time of puberty, just as elementary school teachers need to understand the life body at the time of dentition (the cutting of teeth) around age seven. A study of the seven soul qualities—radiant, shy, life-of-the-party, etc.—in the context of Steiner's pedagogy for adolescence can greatly assist the high school teacher with seating arrangements, instruction, and class discipline. Such insights also provide concrete guidance for grasping Steiner's ideas about the world-soul-moods.

The macrocosmic Platonic year is 25,920 years in length, and each of its twelve ages is 2,160 years in duration, while the microcosmic year is divided into twelve months. Steiner indicated that each of the months has its own virtue connected with the activity of its zodiacal sign which begins on the 21st day of the previous month. For example, the influences of Capricorn—which instills courage and can develop into the power to redeem—begins on December 21st and continues until January 21st. Following Steiner's indications, Waldorf teachers sometimes choose to incorporate these monthly virtues into the regular rhythm of the classroom. For example, a teacher may see the wisdom of becoming a model of courtesy for his or her class at the beginning of the school year.

From August 21st to September 21st, encouraging students to be courteous helps them to unite with the cycle of the year through the influence of Virgo. On September 21st the teacher can begin to model the virtue of contentment, associated with the balanced scale of Libra, which allows him or her to develop equanimity.

Steiner provided detailed introductions to the soul and spiritual nature of the human being in *Knowledge of Higher Worlds* and *Theosophy*, which are known as two of his "basic books."[2] He describes the seven-year cycles of human development using the names of the seven planets, again borrowing the Ptolemaic scheme. Steiner also described the major archetypal experience at the age of twenty-one, the birth of the ego, which ushers in the fourth period of human development—the seven-year cycle of the sentient soul. The first and second seven-year cycles of human development encompass the elementary school years, while high school and the first three years of college complete the third stage of adolescence. As a young adult, the soul quality of the teenage years becomes a world-soul-mood. One of the seven planets spreads its influence over the whole soul life of the individual and forms the inner content of the fire trial, which people of the present age tend to experience outwardly. If individuals do not prepare themselves to meet this trial spiritually, they will move through it nevertheless as a series of life experiences but will necessarily

---

2 For an overview of Steiner's basic books and their relation to his life's work, see my publication *The Basic Books of Rudolf Steiner: A Compact Guide for Individual and Group Study*.

lack a conscious knowledge of its significance for their own personal development.

The same situation obtains in the next seven-year cycle, the water trial, which focuses on the development of the mind soul, also called the intellectual soul. In this cycle, which typically occurs between the ages of twenty-eight through thirty-four, a person develops a worldview—a way of seeing the world from the standpoint of a higher spiritual being—specifically an archai or time spirit that is active in a specific zodiacal sign. An individual can experience this trial of initiation spiritually in an inwardly conscious manner or live through it unconsciously as a series of outer events. The *Mystery Dramas* were Steiner's effort to raise such significant events to waking consciousness through an artistic performance. His lecture cycles on worldviews and world-soul-moods, especially *Human and Cosmic Thought*, provide a complementary pathway to awakening the dormant faculties required to consciously grasp the meaning of such trials that lead to self-knowledge. The goals of the fire trial and the water trial, respectively, are to develop the virtues of common sense and tolerance. Working towards these virtues in a conscious way can lead to deeper personal insight into one's own world soul mood and worldview.

Through these lectures, Steiner provided an additional insight into the twelvefold circles, which each human being is a part of. Each of these circles contains within it three groups of four people, called tones. In astrology, these tones are usually called houses and often consist of four members from a single family, or "royal house." Steiner viewed the three tones as reflections of the influences of the sun, the moon, and the earth and named them theism (thinking), intuitionism (feeling), and naturalism (willing). Against the backdrop of the Platonic year they appear as three squares, with the tone of theism beginning in the sign of Virgo and including Sagittarius, Pisces, and Gemini. Intuitionism forms the square including Leo, Scorpio, Aquarius, and Taurus, while naturalism includes Cancer, Libra, Capricorn, and Aries.

Some explanation of how the twelve members of a karmic circle work together is also necessary. I often follow René Querido and Werner Glas in calling these twelvefold groups "Grail circles."[3] Generally speaking, members who are across the circle from each other, i.e. at a 180-degree angle, are collaborators, while those who are at a 90-degree angle to each other tend to serve as obstacles for each other. Each tone thus contains two pairs of collaborators, but at the same time these two pairs might be at odds with one another and pose obstacles for each other to overcome. The challenge in life, from this viewpoint, is to work for the greater good and to try to take up the mission for the tone as a whole. Practically speaking, each

---

3 I discussed this idea of a karmic circle of twelve characters with two members of the General Council of the Anthroposophical Society in America. Both René Querido and Werner Glas suggested that a careful reading of Shakespeare's plays would reveal a twelvefold grouping of his characters in each of his plays. Some of the research that I have pursued in this direction was incidental to teaching an average of two of the Bard's plays in each of the twenty-seven years I spent as a teacher of high school English classes. Other research was devoted to a specific question: How can the characters of a Shakespeare play be arranged in a Zodiac circle to show the worldview that they represent?

pair of collaborators needs to transform the tendency to obstruct their counterparts into genuine assistance.

In addition to the clockwise movement of the twelve members of a circle through the twelve worldviews, their vertical movement through the seven world-soul-moods (planets), and their arrangement into three tones of four characters each, the twelve members can also be arranged into four elements of three characters each. Whereas the three tones inscribe three squares inside the zodiacal or Grail circle, the four elements inscribe four equilateral triangles inside the circle. In astrology, the zodiacal signs are often discussed according to their associated element as "fire" signs, "air" signs, "water" signs, and "earth" signs. For example, Aries is "fire," Taurus "earth," Gemini "air," and Cancer "water." In the preface to his third mystery drama, Steiner grouped the twelve characters by their elemental sign. His terminology connected fire with spirit, air with soul, water with consecration, and earth with will.

Much research has been done on the Mystery Dramas, especially by the actors, eurythmists, and speech formationists who performed them. One approach that they took up related the theme of initiation in each play to a specific character in that play and identified the ordeals of soul the character underwent. The tone of theism (thinking) contains the four characters whose efforts at self-development were thus highlighted. This house contains Johannas Thomasius, whose trials appear in *The Portal of Initiation*. Also in this house are Maria, whose trials appear in *The Soul's Probation*; Capesius in *The

Guardian of the Threshold; and Strader in *The Soul's Awakening*. The idea of collaborators here finds a fertile area for study. The difficulties that arise for those characters who stand at a right angle to the character experiencing such a trial of soul are also well worth examination.

The tone of naturalism (or willing) contains the four characters who take on the leadership role as hierophants in the sun temple. This house contains Benedictus, Theodosius, Romanus, and Felix. The third tone, intuitionism, contains the remaining characters. Their position in the Grail circle is determined by their elemental sign and tone. Using Steiner's indications in *The Guardian of the Threshold*, the positions of the twelve characters would be as they appear in Chart A.[4]

The Guardian of the Threshold, Steiner's third play, contains the same group of twelve peasants from the second play, *The Soul's Probation*. They have reincarnated from medieval times and their names identify their character traits. Their worldview not only points to the virtues they need to attain, but also to the aspect of their personality in need of development. Chart A includes both the virtues and personality trait of these minor characters along with the worldview of each of the major characters. The world-soul-mood and the tone (or house) in which a character resides may also exert a strong influence on that character's actions and thoughts.

Steiner's first three mystery dramas present two groups of twelve characters who reincarnate in interwoven karmic

---

[4] Steiner's descriptions can be found on pages 7 and 119 of *Four Mystery Dramas*, Steiner Book Centre, Vancouver, Canady 1973.

CHART A

The Circle of Twelve Characters in
The Guardian of the Threshold

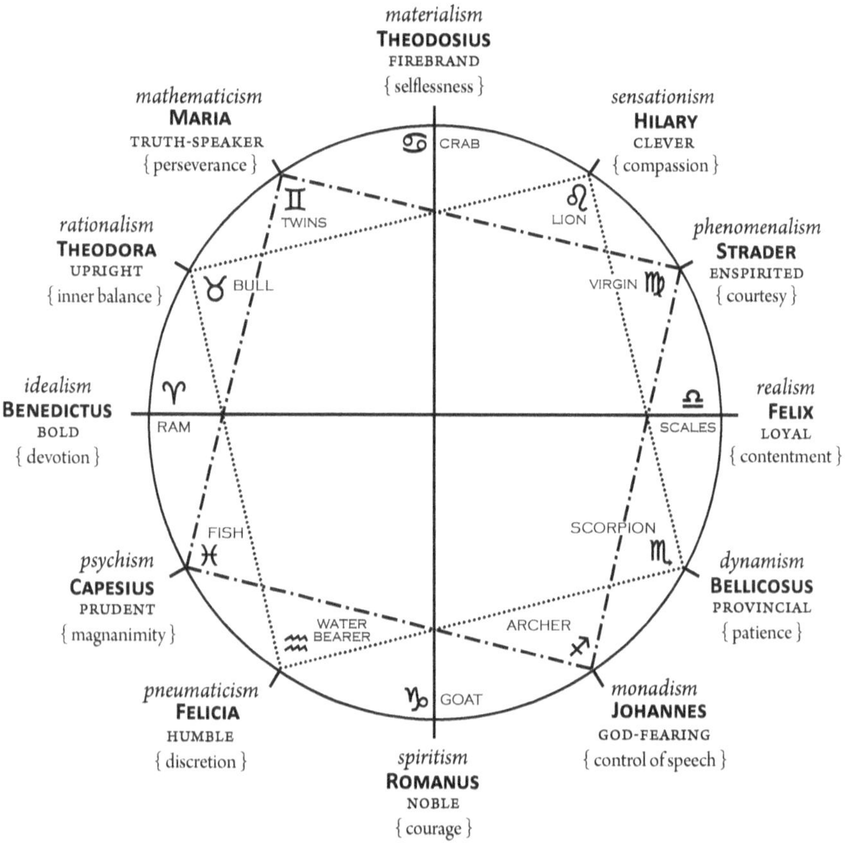
materialism
THEODOSIUS
FIREBRAND
{ selflessness }
sensationism
HILARY
CLEVER
{ compassion }
phenomenalism
STRADER
ENSPIRITED
{ courtesy }
realism
FELIX
LOYAL
{ contentment }
dynamism
BELLICOSUS
PROVINCIAL
{ patience }
monadism
JOHANNES
GOD-FEARING
{ control of speech }
spiritism
ROMANUS
NOBLE
{ courage }
pneumaticism
FELICIA
HUMBLE
{ discretion }
psychism
CAPESIUS
PRUDENT
{ magnanimity }
idealism
BENEDICTUS
BOLD
{ devotion }
rationalism
THEODORA
UPRIGHT
{ inner balance }
mathematicism
MARIA
TRUTH-SPEAKER
{ perseverance }
CRAB
LION
VIRGIN
SCALES
SCORPION
ARCHER
GOAT
WATER BEARER
FISH
RAM
BULL
TWINS

circles. The major characters in scene eleven of the first play and in scenes six through eight of the second play demonstrate the element of destiny in the characters' interactions in the first play by showing certain events of their previous lives in the second play. The continuity of the karmic circles of these twelve individuals is shown in the fourth play, *The Soul's Awakening*, where scene seven—the retrospect into an Egyptian temple in the fifteenth century B.C.—prepares for the initiation in scene eight, which shows the same group of twelve working together. This new form of initiation, emerging for the first time in ancient Egypt, appeared then as blasphemy. It laid the seeds, however, for the great change that initiation was to undergo in later ages.

The Egyptian initiation scene also throws light on later incarnations of this group. Scene seven of *The Portal of Initiation* and scene seven of *The Guardian of the Threshold* show an incarnation in Hibernia (Ireland). The play also presents an incarnation of the karmic circle as the Knights Templar in the fourteenth century—at the beginning of the modern age—in scenes six through eight of *The Soul's Probation*. Maria explains that the medieval incarnation occurred at a turning point in time; thus the positions of the twelve characters in chart A were the same as they had been in the days of Knights Templar. In addition to the Hibernian incarnation, another intervening incarnation probably occurred in ancient Greece. Though Steiner revealed the positions of the twelve characters in the zodiacal circle of the modern age, such indications are lacking for their positions in the zodiacal circle of ancient Egypt. The progress of these individuals in the zodiacal circle since the time of ancient Egypt is unknown, and only further investigation by spiritual researchers would be able to provide further insight.

The second circle of twelve minor characters, who appear as peasants in *The Soul's Probation* and later as the audience for Benedictus's lecture in *The Portal of Initiation*, show how members of a circle can work together as well as create obstacles. In the preface of *The Soul's Awakening*, Steiner indicated that certain characters of the second circle became active in the first circle, for example when Theodora dies and when Capesius becomes ill.

For modern human beings to lead genuine lives and accomplish their goals in freedom, they must know the laws of karma and the truth of reincarnation. Ignorance of reincarnation often means a fear of death. Knowledge of the laws of karma opens insight into each lifetime as the source of a mission for the next incarnation, in which it can be fulfilled. In this light, each person can experience destiny as a gift, chosen by themselves for the sake of further self-development. Steiner's examples show how mean and angry thoughts lead to pain in the next life on earth, and how kind and compassionate thoughts lead to joy.

In 1980, when I began my initial reading of Steiner's lectures on *Karmic Relationships* (CW 235-240), I came across a passage where Steiner described a meeting of Plato and Aristotle in which Plato explained to the younger man that he would need to take up his unfinished work and develop it further—into philosophy. The thought struck me that Steiner could only have written those words if he had been Aristotle in a previous incarnation and had heard this charge himself. The words themselves did not confirm my insight, but its truth only burned brighter. I decided to ask Traute Page about this insight into Steiner's past lives. She would not confirm it, but she did give me a book to read on the condition that I did not copy anything from it or use its contents in any discussions I might have. Since that time, *Rudolf Steiner's Mission and Ita Wegman* by Kirchner-Bockholt has become available to the general public and no longer has to remain under a veil of secrecy. Many excellent biographies of Steiner have been written using Kirchner-Bockholt's information, including an insightful book by Sergei Prokofieff. I would like to build on this body of research by relating Steiner's possible past lives to the zodiacal circle (see Chart B).

In Steiner's incarnation as Aristotle, the birth of philosophy occurred, giving rise to clear thinking grounded in logic. Aristotle's world-soul-mood of logicism aided him in this endeavor. His works of logic still stand today as the foremost expression of the laws of human thinking. Monism also aided him. By uniting concepts and precepts into a whole, Aristotle's scientific works gave rise to a world of knowledge that enabled mankind to survey nature and to create the various scientific fields of knowledge. Pursuing the virtue of control of speech enabled him to attain the feeling for truth—the goal of philosophy. By the nineteenth century, however, this great mission of Aristotle's had succumbed to the danger of materialism— denying God and all other works of the spirit. To counter this

CHART B

The Possible Past Lives of Rudolf Steiner

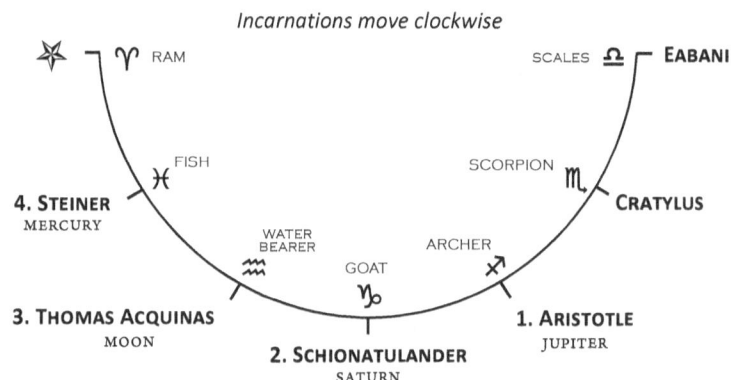

1. **ARISTOTLE** — logicism in monadism
   (Aristotelian philosophy)

2. **SCHIONATULANDER** — gnosticism in spiritism
   (seeking the leash of the dog —
   the Brackenseil, or cosmic script)

3. **THOMAS ACQUINAS** — occultism in pneumatism
   (Dr. Angelicus bringing the Philosopher
   to the Christ Spirit in *Summa Theologica*)

4. **RUDOLF STEINER** — transcendentalism in psychism
   (relating the three soul forces to stages of
   higher knowledge and threefold society)

trajectory, Steiner himself had to experience the soul world and the world of the hierarchies of angels in order to develop a path from natural science to spiritual science. This mission arose for Steiner in his Mars cycle, from age 42 to 49 (1903 to 1910). The founder of philosophy became the founder of Anthroposophy. The transformation of the astral body into the spirit self—the task of the Mars cycle—was here put in the service of writing Anthroposophy's foundational works, the basic books. *Knowledge of the Higher Worlds*, *Theosophy*, and *Occult Science* are the bridge to higher worlds in the present— a rainbow bridge whose light can illumine the human soul. In the corresponding event in the spiritual world, Philosophia rose into the realm of the archangels and became the planetary archangel of the sun—Anthroposophia.[5]

Steiner's medieval incarnation was as the Grail knight Schionatulander. The story of Schionatulander is told in Wolfram von Eschenbach's epic *Parzival*, in which Wolfram showed how Schionatulander served Gahmuret and the mission of uniting the East and the West. After Gahmuret's death in eastern lands, Schionatulander returned to Europe and served Parzival while defending his homeland. He also was in love with Sigune and served her by seeking the collar that granted its possessor access to the cosmic script—the hidden language of the initiates. In his search he came across Orilus, who attacked and slew the unarmed Schionatulander in the mistaken belief that he was Parzival. Even in death, Schionatulander was able to protect

---

5 For a further description of this event, see *The Basic Books of Rudolf Steiner*.

Parzival and help redeem the evil that Parzival's silence had brought to the Grail castle.

In his Mars cycle, Rudolf Steiner reversed the mission of Aristotle by developing a spiritual science to overcome the danger that materialism posed to natural science. By severing ties with the Theosophical Society and denouncing its fraudulent attempt to substitute Krishnamurti for the Second Coming of Christ, he similarly reversed the mission of Schionatulander. In pursuing this second mission, which occurred in his Jupiter cycle from age 49 to 56 (1910 to 1917), Steiner began lecturing about the appearance of the etheric Christ. He also began to design and construct the Goetheanum, creating the imaginative forms of architecture, sculpture, stained-glass, and painting that brought to life this sun-temple of the new mysteries. The transformation of the etheric body into the life spirit—the task of the Jupiter cycle—was placed in service of envisioning the Goetheanum. Schionatulander's etheric body itself actually contained the occult script that he was seeking; Steiner's etheric body now appeared externalized as the House of the Word. Where before Steiner had written books inspired by Anthroposophia, he now created works of art in the service of the Nathan Jesus.

Steiner's following incarnation was Thomas Aquinas, the defender of the faith who opposed the danger of Arabism—an Aristotelianism devoid of the spirit of Christ. The worldview of pneumatism enabled Thomas to experience an individual spiritual being—the Christ—while the world-soul-mood of occultism helped him to develop dormant soul-spirit faculties to experience the hidden God within. Through revelations of Christ's activity in the Bible, Doctor Angelicus could write *Summa Theologica*. The virtue of discretion led him, toward the end of his life at age 48, to observe silence and cease any further expression of his theological views. Steiner indicated that, just as Schionatulander had an important contribution to make toward the mystery stream of Mani, also called the Grail stream, so did Aquinas to the Rosicrucian stream. As the representative of the fourth cultural age of Greece and Rome, he took part in the initiation of Christian Rosenkreutz in the thirteenth century.

A third mission in Rudolf Steiner's life unfolded in the years of 1917 to 1924—his Saturn cycle. Just as Aquinas had opposed Averroes, so did Steiner stand against Woodrow Wilson's Fourteen Points, issued as a proposal for the post-WWI world order in January 1918. Steiner viewed it as an abstract, intellectual proposal stemming from the same source that Acquinas had fought against as a leader of Scholasticism. In its stead he offered a concrete, practical pathway to forming a threefold society. When his ideas fell on deaf ears, he brought new social initiatives into the world in the fields of education, medicine, and agriculture, which are still active a century later. The burning of the Goetheanum on December 31, 1922 revealed the depths of the hatred that Steiner had to face. Less than a year later, he gave his response. At the Christmas Conference of 1923, he presented the Foundation Stone of Love to the 12,000 members of the Anthroposophical Society and to the world. The transformation of the physical body into spirit man—the task of the Saturn cycle—was then put into the service of Michael through the founding of the Michael School, the esoteric core of the new Anthroposophical Society, which Steiner himself united with by becoming its president. The founder of Anthroposophy and the creator of the Goetheanum now became a Master of Wisdom, the co-equal of Christian Rosenkreutz, who together served as leaders of the Michael School. This last sacrifice resulted in his illness and death in 1925.

The central theme of this book on the mystery stream of Parzival in the twentieth century —the Grail stream—requires a certain clarity about reincarnation and Masters of Wisdom such as Christian Rosenkreutz. In one sense, working towards such clarity was the all-encompassing goal of Rudolf Steiner's life. He developed a science of the spirit as the counterpoint to what Aristotle had brought into the world—a natural science based in logic that would enable mankind to understand the physical world around him. A corresponding science of the spirit—a spiritual science—that applies the same logic and common-sense understanding to the "unseen" world is essential in order for mankind to be truly free and able to judge events correctly.

In *Rudolf Steiner and the Masters of Esoteric Christianity*, Sergei Prokofieff assembled Steiner's indications on this difficult topic and helped bring the needed clarity. Certain key ideas of Prokofieff can shed light on eight important historical figures, whom I will take up in detail, along with their circles of co-workers. Prokofieff's book is long, and my attempt to

CHAPTER I   23

shorten and summarize his discussions of the four key thoughts is not conclusive. Rather, it is an effort to characterize the spiritual background of these individuals and the times they lived in, through which I hope to bring these historical figures alive.

The idea of masters—more correctly, Masters of Wisdom and the Harmony of Feelings—recalls the basic idea of this book: that there are twelve zodiacal signs and twelve human beings in a zodiacal group. The masters are generally called bodhisattvas, or "human bodhisattvas," who rise up to Buddhahood in their final incarnation. Siddhartha Gautama was the most recent bodhisattva to attain Buddhahood. He did so in the sixth century B.C. and became the sixth Ascended Master. Six more must make this ascension before the goal of earthly evolution is achieved. A great part of mankind will by then have perfected their character and be able to join with the Ascended Masters as the tenth class in the angelic hierarchies. Prokofieff explained that Ascended Masters can also be called Eastern Masters, who help mankind from spiritual realms but no longer incarnate. Western Masters are different in that they continually incarnate, not only in the one incarnation in which they attain to Buddhahood. As is the case of Steiner, they have many full incarnations. Bernard Lievegoed's book, *The Battle for the Soul*, also discusses the various incarnations of Parzival and Christian Rosenkreutz, as well as those of Rudolf Steiner.

The missions of those three Western Masters are bound up with the second key concept of this book—the New Jerusalem. "The Revelations of St. John" in the *Bible* describes how the New Jerusalem will look in the future when it is completed. Wolfram's *Parzival* describes how it looked in the ninth century, when it was known as the Grail Castle. When Parzival became Lord of the Grail in 869 A.D., he formed the first foundation stone. Becoming a Grail knight was no easy task, as King Arthur and his noble knights discovered. *The Chymical Wedding of Christian Rosenkreutz* tells of Rosenkreutz's initiation in the fifteenth century, which led to the second foundation stone—the Philosopher's Stone, or stone of the wise. Other Western Masters joined with Rosenkreutz. In small groups, meeting in secrecy, they actively developed this path more fully. The foundation stone laid by Rudolf Steiner was different. The stone of love was open for all to see, and even the nineteen mantras of the first class of the Michael School are now as available as one of his basic books. Only dedicated group work will create the future building as envisioned, but that work need no longer be conducted in secret societies. Gradually, the unity of all religions on earth will become a visible reality. At first this insight will manifest as an inner conviction, gradually to emerge externally and ennoble daily life.

The third key concept connected to the Western Masters and the New Jerusalem is that of the Spirit of Truth—the source of that ennoblement and the basis for such unity. When Christ spoke of it, he told his disciples that they should not bemoan and grieve over His crucifixion; only so could He send them the Advocate, the Paraclete—the Spirit of Truth. He also intimated its connection to the Baptism with fire, with the

Holy Spirit. Grasping this idea concretely requires becoming familiar with the hierarchy of angels—from angels (guardian spirits of individuals), archangels (group souls), archai (time spirits), and six further classes. Only then can the activity of the Godhead be dimly sensed: the Holy Spirit through the spirits of soul (angels, archangels, and archai), and the Son and Father through the second and first hierarchies.

The Spirit of Truth, as Prokofieff explained, is an avatar—a group of three or more angels, archangels, and archai. The composite spiritual being yet acts as a single being. It is able to work simultaneously into the physical body, the life body, and the soul body of a human being. This activity is the secret of the spiritual power in the Buddha when he was under the bodhi tree. A human bodhisattva may be a great leader of mankind, but the twelve divine bodhisattvas—the twelve spirits of truth—are the actual basis for the grouping of human beings into circles of twelve. They stand behind the twelve tribes and other such groups mentioned earlier. These avatars can work through human bodhisattvas to bring birth to new faculties that all mankind can then develop. These Spirits of Truth can inspire human bodhisattvas and through them a whole community of like-minded men and women. In the coming chapters various leaders will speak at one time or another of the Blessed Community. Rather than bemoan the transitory appearance and ephemeral nature of such communities, they should be seen as harbingers—signs of the next age of human culture which is called in "The Revelations of St. John" by the name of Philadelphia, the city of Brotherly Love.

I first lectured on the relation of three spiritual beings to the development of the three higher members of Steiner's spiritual being in 2001. It was not until 2019 that, in reading Prokofieff's book, I could find a kind of confirmation for the use I had made of the Kirchner-Bockholt book at that time. The idea of seeing those three members of the third hierarchy as a composite being—an avatar—and the spiritual basis for identifying Steiner as a Western Master was Prokofieff's.

Another viewpoint may help clarify the circle of twelve people who surrounded Steiner. In particular, the birth of philosophy in ancient Greece sheds light on the collaborators and obstacles that Aristotle faced at that time. In discussing Steiner's incarnation as Aristotle, an attempt was made to explain his worldview of monadism and his world-soul-mood of logicism and how they assisted Aristotle in founding philosophy. Steiner also discussed Plato's dualism, which can be connected with Gemini and mathematicism. Plato even inscribed the words "Let none but geometricians enter here" on the portal to his Academy. Plato's dialogues are related to Mercury—the world-soul-mood of transcendentalism, or the coordinated thinking of dialectics. Aristotle's task was to move from the atmosphere of mystery wisdom to the earthbound thinking of modern human beings. In terms of the tone of theism (the house of philosophy), Plato was in Gemini and Aristotle in Sagittarius. They collaborated in the founding of philosophy. *The Mission of Rudolf Steiner and Ita Wegman* clearly states that Aristotle and Alexander worked together—that they were in the same tone—but that Alexander caused Aristotle many difficulties and became an obstacle for him. This problem persisted down to the present time. Socrates was the fourth member of the tone of theism (the sun influence in the realm of thinking, as was appropriate for the founding of philosophy). He began this process by gathering around himself disciples like Plato to carry out what he viewed to be his duty to the oracle of Apollo. Plato hallowed it by bringing it into the precincts of the Academy. Aristotle perfected it in his walks in the Lyceum, and Alexander spread it by founding schools of philosophy in the East.

In his third incarnation after Aristotle, Steiner again entered the world tone of theism. He was again united with Ita Wegman, as he had been in all five of his earlier incarnations. Prokofieff points out that this fact did not imply that he had been initiated in any of those previous incarnations. Prokofieff also suggested that Steiner collaborated with the reincarnated Plato—Karl Julius Schroer. The Goethe task, as Steiner referred to it, began when he was twenty-one years old with the offer of Joseph Kurschner to edit Goethe's scientific work for the *German National Literature* edition. By 1884, Steiner completed volume one of Goethe's *Scientific Writings* (CW1). By 1886, the director of the Goethe Archive in Weimar invited Steiner's collaboration. Steiner completed two more volumes of Goethe's scientific writing before moving to Weimar in 1890. He worked there until 1896, publishing *Goethe's Worldview* (CW6) the following year. His determination to complete a mission that essentially belonged to Schroer strangely echoes the debt that Aristotle owed to the Academy and Plato's instruction in the same period of his life in ancient Athens. The fourth member of the ancient Greek tone of theism, the house of philosophy, also reincarnated in Europe in the nineteenth century—Leo Tolstoy. His fame was vast, but his connection to the house of anthroposophy, as it could be called, is not as straightforward as the other three members.

Prokofieff discussed Steiner's mission of bringing a spiritually scientific and logical conception of reincarnation into the modern age. He related it to the mission of Aristotle who "fully rejected the idea of reincarnation in order thereby to strengthen in human beings the forces of the individual ego that were necessary for them to be able subsequently to receive the Christ impulse." The result was the disappearance of this idea from Western culture. By what Prokofieff called the law of repetition (the same individual must fulfill a single task—albeit in two opposite directions), required its return in a new Christian form in the present age.

When I lectured on Ralph Waldo Emerson's missions, I used his characterization of this law, which he called the law of bias, or polarity. Every soul has a unique mission, he observed, for "everyone is a magnet with a new north." The task is singular and belongs to one person alone. All other tasks can find co-workers, helpers, and collaborators, but this task experiences opposition and discouragement at every turn. Persistence above all is required if it is to be achieved, for all people and situations seem to conspire against its fulfillment. For Emerson this mission was to write the *Natural History of the Intellect*, a work that he considered the chief task of his life and worked on diligently over the course of thirty-three years, though it became largely unknown after his death. One knows the task clearly since it is what one loves the most. Only such devotion can bring its completion. Steiner speaks of his mission to bring the idea of reincarnation alive in the present age in a way similar way. It is the one task forever pushed aside. He finally accomplished it in 1925, his last year of worldly activity.

2.
Abraham Lincoln and the Civil War

In the same year that I had had an experience of Rudolf Steiner's past life as Aristotle, I came across a passage in Steiner's lecture cycle, *The Gospel of St. Mark* (CW 139), that affected me in an equally powerful fashion. Steiner stated that Hamlet was the reincarnation of the Trojan hero Hector. I had majored in English, and in my senior year of college the topic I chose for my senior thesis was *Hamlet*. Shakespeare's greatness can be compared to that of Homer, Virgil, Dante, and Goethe. Taking up the theme of the anxiety of meaninglessness in one of Shakespeare's most important plays was certainly beyond my depth, but it seemed worth the effort. Graduation requirements included proficiency in a foreign language. Since taking up a new language seemed too difficult, I continued my high school work in Latin and took Latin 1a in college. I spent a year translating Virgil's *Aeneid* and Ovid's *Metamorphoses*.

Steiner's indication about Hamlet's earlier life as Hector gave a new and deeper meaning to Hamlet's request of the First Player for a recitation of "The Death of Priam." The recitation led to Hamlet's decision to catch the conscience of King Claudius. By performing "The Mousetrap," the Players would be re-enacting the murder of King Hamlet by his brother, Claudius. The scene, from Virgil's *Aeneid* included six characters: Aeneas, who watched from his hiding place; Hector's ghost, who had guided Aeneas in an attempt to help him escape the downfall of Troy; Pyrrhus, who broke into the king's chamber; King Priam, who unsheathed his sword in a feeble attempt to defend himself; and Queen Hecuba and Helen, who looked on helplessly as Pyrrhus slaughtered the Trojan king. The corresponding scene two millennia later appeared in *Hamlet* as "The Mousetrap." Horatio (the reincarnated Aeneas) stood and watched the play, while Hamlet (the reborn Hector) sat and watched with Ophelia (the reborn Helen) at his side. King Claudius (the reincarnated Pyrrhus) also watched the play, which re-enacted his poisoning of King Hamlet (the reborn Priam). In the light of "The Death of Priam," Claudius carried the guilt of two murders. When Claudius screamed for light, he made it clear that the mousetrap had been sprung and that it had succeeded in catching the conscience of the king. Queen Gertrude (the reborn Queen Hecuba) sat with her husband's murderer and watched the play, but missed its deeper meaning. When Hamlet discussed its meaning with her later that night, she finally awoke to the truth of her situation.

As I had done with my insight into Steiner's past life, I took the question of the validity of my view about the past lives of the characters in *Hamlet* to Dr. Traute Page. She recommended that I write a letter to Friedrich Hiebel, a leader of the Anthroposophical Society whose headquarters was in Switzerland. His reply did confirm my insight into the past lives of the six characters mentioned above, though he stated that he was too busy to engage in any further correspondence on the subject.

Fortunately, other Anthroposophical researchers had taken up the study of *Hamlet*. I have mentioned Werner Glas and René Querido previously in connection with the idea that each of the Bard's plays contained a Grail circle of twelve characters. René also suggested that I pursue an insight of Steiner's: that *Hamlet* holds the same position in the English-speaking world that *Faust* does in the German speaking-world. He then indicated that the source of Hamlet's skepticism and doubt derived from his teacher at Wittenberg—Faust himself. Steiner had also contradicted the common view that the events in *Hamlet* were not historical. His research indicated that they in fact were. When the BBC commemorated the four hundredth anniversary of Shakespeare's birth by filming productions of all thirty-six of his plays, they staged *Hamlet* in the castle of Elsinore in Denmark.

René suggested that I read a book written by an Anthroposophist whose research on *Hamlet* had been published. Madge Childs wrote *Hamlet: Through the Valley of the Shadow*, which showed concretely that *Hamlet* was a further development of the Greek tragedies. She explained how the lesser mysteries of antiquity had become the modern trials of initiation. Hamlet's fire trial involved the appearance of his father's ghost and the command to avenge his death. Hamlet's water trial required him to sail to England and learn the occult script. His attainment of this is symbolized by his rewriting of the commission that he was to give to the English king. Lastly, his air trial occurred during the duel with Laertes.

Childs's book also took up the archetypes connected with each of the twelve characters in *Hamlet* and related them to the characters in Goethe's "The Fairy Tale of the Green Snake and the Beautiful Lily." The research that I had already done on the relation of Steiner's characters in the first mystery drama, *The Portal of Initiation*, to Goethe's fairy tale helped to clarify the three houses (or tones) in *Hamlet*. The house of Hamlet (the tone of theism, or thinking) included King Hamlet and wife, Queen Gertrude. Those collaborators stood at right angles to Prince Hamlet (to whom Gertrude had become a stumbling block) and Claudius (who stole the King's wife and crown and who, as the son of Achilles, had come into the royal house of the Troy by being held back after his ancient Greece incarnation). The house of Fortinbras (the tone of naturalism, or willing) included King Fortinbras, young Fortinbras, and his captain. Horatio had been closely connected to Hector, but it was the initiation of Aeneas that pushed him forward into the royal house of Norway and held Pyrrhus back so that he entered the royal house of Denmark. The house of Polonius (the tone of intuitionism, or feeling) contained Polonius, Paris, and Helen, though the latter two—who had been deemed to be the cause of the Trojan War—were now brother and sister. The two brothers, Menelaus and Agamemnon—who had held the suitors to their word at Aulis—were now Polonius and old Norway, chief advisers of their respective kings and determined to keep the peace.

I did not arrive at the chart of the twelve central characters in *Hamlet* (chart C) overnight. The discussion of the three

CHART C

The Three Tones in Shakespeare's *Hamlet*

	HOUSE OF **HAMLET** *theism - sun* ☉	HOUSE OF **POLONIUS** *intuitionism - moon* ☾	HOUSE OF **FORTINBRAS** *naturalism - earth* ⊕
NORTH	**Prince Hamlet**	**Laertes**	**Prince Fortinbras**
EAST	**King Hamlet**	**Old Norway**	**King Fortinbras**
SOUTH	**Claudius**	**Ophelia**	**Horatio**
WEST	**Gertrude**	**Polonius**	**Captain**

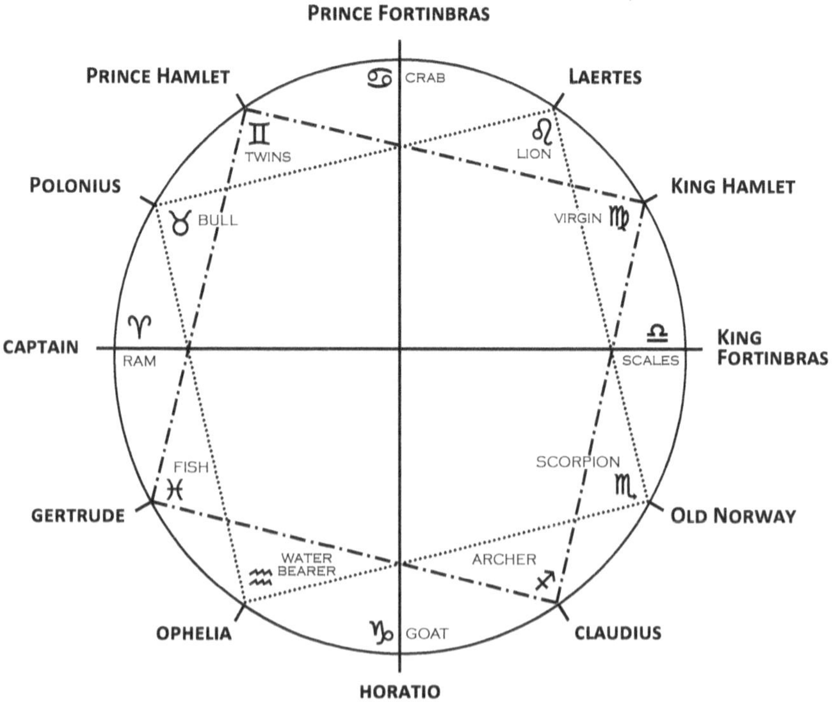

houses in *Hamlet* could be greatly expanded, and a separate examination of the four elements mentioned earlier would be helpful as well. Such insight into the worldviews and personalities of these characters would be important for an actor or director to know. That Hamlet stands in the zodiacal sign of the truth-speaker and Ophelia in the sign of humility, and that they share the element of water (or consecration), would help to confirm Shakespeare's greatness, not lessen it.

The reason forty years had to elapse before I could publish these findings had to do with the fact that, from the very beginning, I felt that there had to be one—and maybe more—intervening incarnations of these individuals between ancient Greece and medieval Denmark. Steiner did make clear that the themes of *The Iliad* and of *Hamlet* were the same. The shades of the Trojan War were active in *Hamlet* because each war was fought to bring to an end the decadence of a specific mystery center. The Eastern mysteries wished to sustain their hold on power through the patriarchy embodied in King Priam, while the upstart civilization in Greece sought to introduce the ideal of freedom and the dignity of the individual to the world. *The Iliad* begins with an argument between the Greek king and Achilles that results in Achilles's disobedience to the king and his refusal to fight. The rottenness in Denmark was due to the decadence of the Northern mysteries—the evil that Hamlet was born to set right.

Some similar research that I was working on led me to consider an event in Roman history as a possible intervening incarnation. This event fell midway between the time of the

Trojan War, which archeologists date around 1250 B.C., and that of the war between Norway and Denmark, which the education that Laertes received in the French kingdom would suggest to have occurred during the time of Charlemagne—around 800 A.D. More importantly, the theme of the decadent Southern mysteries would point to the great obstacle that Rome would face in its attempt to bring Roman law onto the stage of world history.

Roman historians did take up the question of the significance of the Punic Wars, a series of three wars lasting over a hundred years from 264 B.C. to 146 B.C. Livy's histories are the best-known source of the battle plans and strategy of the Carthaginian army that opposed Rome's hegemony over Sicily. The decadence of the Southern mysteries is more clearly apparent in the epic written by Selius Italicus, the *Punica*. The Carthaginian ruling house and its king, Hamilcar Barca, played important roles, but his son, Hannibal, became Rome's nemesis in the Second Punic War. Scipio was the Roman general who finally defeated him, gaining the title of Africanus in the process. Scipio also brought the Palladium to Rome, which guaranteed Rome's victory, just as Odysseus had secured the Greek victory by stealing the Palladium from Troy to bring about its destruction.

Plutarch's *Parallel Lives of Famous Greek and Romans* provides the key information for any attempt to relate these Romans and Carthaginians to the twelve historical figures who first appeared in the epics of Homer and Virgil and afterwards in Shakespeare's *Hamlet*. Plutarch's biographies explore the moral qualities and character of his numerous subjects, supported by concrete historical events and detailed comparisons with similar historical figures. Three of his biographies are helpful in grasping the House of Atreus and its transition into the House of Polonius. The biography of Flamininus (230-174 B.C.) reveals the reckless selfishness of Paris. The personality of the firebrand, characteristic of the sign of Cancer, will shift to cleverness in his incarnation as Laertes when the trick he plans with the help of Claudius culminates with Hamlet's demise. The biography of Fabius (270-203 B.C.) shows his complete loyalty to Rome, the quality bound up with the sign of Libra. The enspirited King of the Greek army, Agamemnon, was tricked by Zeus's lying dream into believing that he could defeat Hector without the aid of Achilles. He refused to be fooled a second time. He became Fabius the Delayer. He refused to engage Hannibal, perhaps instinctively sensing that Troy's greatest hero was wreaking his revenge on the souls of those who had once sacked Troy. In an ironic twist, Rome was not protected by a massive wall, as Troy had been. Rather, the Roman army's general, Fabius, knew full well that only the army's defeat at the hands of Hannibal would leave Rome defenseless. The tens of thousands of old men, women and children would have happily fought an invading army to the death—a kind of Roman Sparta with a race of warriors.

The third biography was about the life of Marcellus (268-208 B.C.). Refusing to take Fabius's advice to delay, he exhibited the boldness inherent in the sign of Aries by following Hannibal's army in the hope of winning a decisive battle.

The ingenious ambush that Hannibal arranged cost Marcellus his life. A similar mistake (though with a reversal) resulted in Polonius's demise while he was hiding in Gertrude's closet. What had been the House of Atreus at the time of the Trojan War simply shifted one zodiacal sign at the time of the second Punic War and entered the tone of naturalism. The willing aspect of this tone might justify calling it the House of the Roman Generals. The house of Priam, on the other hand, had one member, Aeneas, whose initiation caused him to shift two zodiacal signs and enter what had been the House of the Greek Heroes, but in Roman times was called the House of Scipio. Scipio Africanus, his brother Lucius, and Aemilianus Scipio were joined by Marcus Cato. Plutarch's biography of Cato shows how extraordinary this god-fearing man was. His destiny saved him from engaging in battle against Hannibal.

Owing to the initiation of Aeneas, Pyrrhus, who was also called Neoptolemus, was held back in the tone of intuitionism and then entered the House of Priam, against whom he had committed such sacrilege. Antiochus was not a blood member of the House of Barca; rather he was more like a strange ally in their war against Rome. In his following incarnation, he became the brother of King Hamlet, the villainous Claudius. This idea of initiation causes havoc for the other members belonging to the circle of the one who advances. Confusion also emanates from the individual who remains stationary. Steiner pointed out to those who wish to set foot on such a path that they need to be clear about their responsibility to help others. The idea of initiation was not unknown to the

Romans. Plutarch discussed it in connection with many of his biographies. The central event in the *Aeneid* is the journey of Aeneas to the Underworld. In the Elysian Field, Aeneas—the Trojan hero who will help in the founding of Rome—met his father. Anchises told him the secret of reincarnation—that human beings yearn to return to an earthly life after many years in eternal worlds and then they drink from the river Lethe, the river of Forgetfulness, before experiencing the upper world in a new life. This founding epic of Roman culture, which every literate Roman was expected to read, also had Anchises inform his son that the heroes of ancient Greece and the Trojan war had been incarnating in Rome down to the time of Caesar Augustus.

Working with insights into reincarnation like those of Steiner or those of Kirchner-Bockholt, who was reporting about Steiner's insights, puts the researcher into the position of a scientist who needs to construct an experiment in an attempt to prove his hypothesis. Such proof cannot make the hypothesis true, but only provide more evidence and support for its likelihood. Examining the possible past lives of Steiner and gaining more facts about them can allow the character, worldview, and mission of each individual to emerge. Such characterizations make the likelihood of their being one and the same individual ego ever greater. The same method can apply to Steiner's insight that Hamlet was a reincarnation of Hector. My research that was done in college was certainly helpful and encouraging, but much more needed to be done. Steiner's idea about the decadent mysteries led me to the possibility of the Punic War as an intervening incarnation. Without an authority like Plutarch, the lack of sufficient evidence about the character, worldview, and mission of each Roman general would have greatly reduced the likelihood of their being an intervening incarnation of the Greek heroes. Just as a scientist publishes his work for others to take up, so does the spiritual scientist.

On November 24, 1998, another insight struck me. It concerned research I had been doing on the American Civil War as a member of an Anthroposophical interest group that had taken up the study of religious sects and other spiritual groups in America. One evening while studying Frederick Douglass's autobiography, I experienced a repetition of Aeneas's escape from Troy. The next morning, I wrote down Aeneas along with the eleven other Trojan and Greek heroes in the zodiacal circle of the Trojan War and drew their connection to various Confederate and Union participants in the American Civil War. Fortunately, important biographies had been written on most of the Civil War leaders. The autobiographies of Douglass, Grant, and Sherman proved to be as helpful as Plutarch's *Lives* in clarifying each of their life cycles, character, and worldview. By the fall of 2000, I began lecturing on Lincoln and other Civil War leaders. I wrote a draft of a book on them in 2009, though without an explanation of reincarnation such as this book attempts to provide, I did not feel comfortable editing and publishing it.

The main reason to consider the possibility of the reincarnation of Greek and Trojan heroes in Roman times can be found in Virgil's *Aeneid*, as mentioned previously. Steiner indicated that *Hamlet* was a repetition of the fall of Troy and of the decadent mysteries. Slavery in the United States can similarly be viewed as a sign of the decadence of the Western mysteries. Certain Western secret societies maintained that rulership over the present age was the birthright of the Anglo-Saxon race. They spread this doctrine of white supremacy through the Ku Klux Klan and other occult groups that employed the misuse of certain powers, such as mass hypnosis, for selfish and nationalistic purposes.

The chart of the Civil War leaders (chart D) shows three houses or tones. The tone of theism (or thinking) includes those who were in the same tone in ancient Greece—the House of Atreus. How ironic that those who once fought for the Greek ideal of freedom were now trying to preserve slavery. Agamemnon, however, was no longer in that house—his place being taken by Pyrrhus, who was held back in ancient Greece and again in medieval Denmark. The evil that John Wilkes Booth represented suggests that he may have belonged to those western secret societies that engage in assassination. The picture of Lincoln at the Ford Theatre watching a play, which symbolically told the story of his life, while Booth shot him from behind, is a precise reversal of the performance of "The Mousetrap" in *Hamlet*.

The tone of intuitionism (or feeling) in chart D is basically composed of those who were in the House of Priam at the time of the Trojan War. The three who experienced initiation at that time were able to advance and enter the House of

CHART D

The Circle of Twelve Civil War Leaders and Their Three Houses (or Tones)

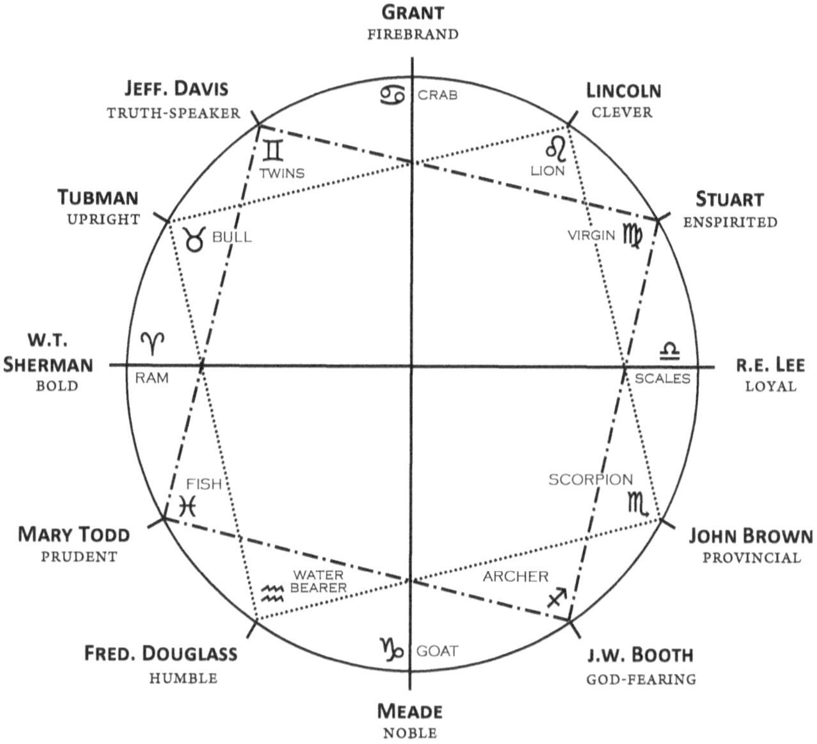

- **GRANT** — FIREBRAND (♋ CRAB)
- **JEFF. DAVIS** — TRUTH-SPEAKER (♊ TWINS)
- **LINCOLN** — CLEVER (♌ LION)
- **TUBMAN** — UPRIGHT (♉ BULL)
- **STUART** — ENSPIRITED (♍ VIRGIN)
- **W.T. SHERMAN** — BOLD (♈ RAM)
- **R.E. LEE** — LOYAL (♎ SCALES)
- **MARY TODD** — PRUDENT (♓ FISH)
- **JOHN BROWN** — PROVINCIAL (♏ SCORPION)
- **FRED. DOUGLASS** — HUMBLE (♒ WATER BEARER)
- **J.W. BOOTH** — GOD-FEARING (♐ ARCHER)
- **MEADE** — NOBLE (♑ GOAT)

	CONFEDERATES sun - thinking ☉	EMANCIPATORS moon - feeling ☾	GENERALS earth - willing ⊕
NORTH	JEFF. DAVIS	ABRAHAM LINCOLN	U.S. GRANT
EAST	J.E.B. STUART	JOHN BROWN	R.E. LEE
SOUTH	J.W. BOOTH	FREDERICK DOUGLASS	MEADE
WEST	MARY TODD	HARRIET TUBMAN	SHERMAN

the Emancipators to join with the one remaining Greek hero, Odysseus. The biography *The Giants* by John Stauffer represents an important attempt to characterize the renewal of the collaboration of Hector and Aeneas, as well as that of Hamlet and Horatio. The publication of Lincoln's Emancipation Proclamation on January 1, 1863 led to Douglass's assembling recruits for the 54th and 55th Massachusetts regiments. Shortly before his death, Lincoln brought forth the 13th amendment, which abolished slavery, while Douglass took up the struggle for Civil Rights that abolition entailed and helped to pass the 14th and 15th amendments. John Brown and Harriet Tubman have not yet found chroniclers to tell their stories aright, but their sacrifices were equally as sublime as those of Lincoln and Douglass.

The tone of naturalism (or willing) includes the one remaining member of the House of Priam, Robert E. Lee. Two members of the House of the Greek heroes had been held back to oppose General Lee. They were joined by a member of the House of Atreus who had advanced, General Meade. It was Meade who defeated Lee at Gettysburg simply by holding the high ground and fending off the futile attacks of the Confederate troops. Ever the Delayer, Meade refused to follow up and pursue the beaten Lee, and Lincoln promptly replaced him. Both Ulysses S. Grant and William Sherman wrote memoirs that explained their military strategy in detail. In addition, President Lincoln ordered the War Department to make all its files open to the public. Grant's memoir holds a special place for the historian. Like Plutarch, he had the master historian's uncanny knack for recognizing the moral qualities and character of friend and foe alike. He shared his insights and showed the source of his military genius.

Characterizing Rudolf Steiner's past lives can shed a certain light on the seven-year cycles of his life in the twentieth century. In a similar way, Abraham Lincoln's past lives can reveal his worldview, world-soul-mood, character, as well as his missions. The same is true for Frederick Douglass. Each one received an initiation: Douglass in the course of his life as Aeneas, and Lincoln in his life as Hamlet. They each journeyed through two worldviews in those lives as well as two world-soul-moods. Just as it is helpful to know that Steiner was in logicism (Jupiter) in his Aristotle incarnation, so is knowing that Lincoln was in Transcendentalism (Mercury) in his Hannibal incarnation, and that Douglass was in mysticism in his Horatio incarnation.

Only by grasping character aright can one avoid becoming a pawn or puppet in the struggle between two mighty opposites. In *Hamlet* these opposing forces are personified by Hamlet and Claudius. Shakespeare's genius tears away the fog of confusion and mists of rhetoric to reveal the truth-speaker in Hamlet and the evil in Claudius. *Hamlet* occurred on earth as a world historic event. Being on the right side of history requires a profound grasp of the true character of these mighty forces.

Shakespeare's characters are considered to be rounded and true-to-life. Steiner even said about them that they were more real and alive than many people walking down the street, who now lead such superficial lives. Shakespeare's plots are equally amazing. Find the climax of a play written by the Bard and list six to twelve events in the prologue and rising action, then list their corresponding events in the falling action and conclusion. I have given such an assignment to high school students after reading and discussing a Shakespearean tragedy in class. I would ask them to choose two pairs of events and explain in a paragraph how the second event in the pair is both a repetition and a reversal of the first one. I always discovered that the class as a whole found more pairs than I had found, and that some of their insights were deeper than those of their teacher.

The plot of *Hamlet* bears a certain similarity to the events of both the Trojan War and the American Civil War. In Act 1, Scene 1 of *Hamlet*, the audience is told the reason for the enmity that Norway held towards Denmark. A dispute over land had arisen that was settled by a duel between the two monarchs. King Hamlet won the duel and the disputed lands, and King Fortinbras was slain. A similar dispute stood behind the Trojan War. Heracles held the king of Troy responsible for not paying a debt, invaded his city, and killed King Lemedon. Historians generally trace the origins of the Civil War back to the Kansas-Nebraska Act of 1854, which brought John Brown to "Bleeding" Kansas. Brown's opposition to slavery sent him to Harper's Ferry in an attempt to start a slave rebellion there in 1859. Robert E. Lee captured him, and he was hung in December of that year. Odysseus apparently was quite insistent in trying to make up for the trick of the Trojan Horse. He sacrificed himself twice to King Priam, first by reincarnating as King Fortinbras and losing to King Hamlet in a duel, and then by reincarnating as John Brown and being captured by Robert E. Lee.

The second event of the prologue of *Hamlet* occurred in Act 1, Scene 2. The marriage of Queen Gertrude and Claudius horrified Hamlet. The evil it represented echoed the event that had caused the Trojan War—the abduction of Helen by Paris. The idea that Helen was the bearer of the spirit of Greece can be found in Euripides's play, *Helen*. The deed that actually triggered the American Civil War repeated the evil of Paris. The spirit of America was abducted when the Confederacy seceded from the Union. How ironic that the reborn Menelaus—Jefferson Davis—became the president of the Confederate States and did to America what had been done to him.

The final event of the prologue can also be viewed as the first turning point of the plot. In scene five of the first act, Prince Hamlet meets the ghost of his father, hears the story of his murder, and takes an oath to avenge King Hamlet's murder. Madge Childs suggested a deeper meaning of the call for vengeance, one in keeping with the idea of awakening the killer's conscience.[6] The event in the Punic War that corresponds to this oath of Hamlet occurred when Hamilcar took Hannibal to a mountain near Carthage and required his young son to take an oath that he would destroy Rome completely. In light of their connection to the King and Prince of Troy, Hamilcar was obviously demanding that Hannibal carry out revenge in its literal meaning. The oath taken by the suitors of Helen is the antecedent of the oath taken by Hamlet. The

---

6 Madge Childs, *Hamlet: Through the Valley of the Shadow*.

suitors of Helen fulfilled their oath by gathering at Aulis to begin an expedition that took ten years to complete. The idea of protecting Helen referred equally to the Spirit of Greece that overshadowed her. In a similar way, the Founding Fathers did not view the Constitution as a piece of paper, but as a home for the spirit of liberty, the spirit of America, whom they called Columbia. The oath that Lincoln took in 1861 to uphold and defend the Constitution of the United States was akin to the oath of the suitors.

The first event of the rising action of *Hamlet* occurs in Act 2, Scene 1. Hamlet visits Ophelia in the hope of finding her sympathetic to his plight, but she is frightened by his strange behavior and even thinks that he might have gone mad. In the Trojan war, Achilles travelled to the ten smaller cities that surrounded Troy and conquered the Decapolis, but his victories did not sway the Trojans to cease their resistance to the Greek army. In the Civil War, the Union army entered into Confederate Virginia, but the First Battle of Manasses, also called the Battle of Bull Run, did not shake the will of the Army of Northern Virginia. It was there that General Jackson earned his nickname of Stonewall.

The next event in *Hamlet* showed that Claudius was far more worried about Hamlet's behavior than about the danger posed by Norway's army. Claudius accepts the peace offering of old Norway, but discusses schemes with Rosencrantz, Guildenstern, and Polonius that might enable him to discover whether Hamlet posed a real threat. His unstated fear was that Hamlet somehow knew the truth about his own treachery.

Homer's epic, *The Iliad*, began *in media res* ("in the middle of things") with the confusion in the Greek ranks that arose from the quarrel between King Agamemnon and the leader of the Greek army, Achilles. Just as the Danish king could not get the prince to cooperate, so too did King Agamemnon fail to get Achilles to follow his orders. The furious Achilles left the meeting sulking, a god holding his hand to prevent regicide. President Lincoln faced similar insubordination from his generals. In response, the reincarnated Hannibal spent the following months studying military strategy through aid of his access to the Library of Congress.

In the last scene of Act 2 and first scene of Act 3, Claudius sent his spies to interrogate Hamlet and even eavesdropped himself on Hamlet's conversation with Ophelia. These verbal skirmishes took the place of the actual military operations that had occurred during the Trojan War. Hector led the Trojans against the Greek armies and defeated them soundly, driving them back to their ships and even setting fire to some of them. His victory included the killing of Patroclus, who had donned Achilles's black armor in an attempt to inspire the Greeks and scare the Trojans into believing the leader of the Greeks had joined the fray. Like Hannibal's defeats of the Roman armies in Italy, Hector struck fear in all who opposed him. Robert E. Lee attained a similar status as leader of the Army of Northern Virginia. With Generals Longstreet and Jackson, he defeated every attempt of the Army of the Potomac to invade the Confederacy and capture its capital in Richmond.

The climax of *Hamlet* is the performance of "The Mousetrap." This event is a repetition of "The Death of Priam" in *The Aeneid*, and it was repeated a third time when Lincoln was assassinated. This climax is also connected with the climax of the Trojan War, which occurred when Odysseus, with the help of Helen, stole the talisman that protected Troy, the Palladium. This talisman played a similar role in the Punic Wars when the reincarnated Odysseus travelled to Athens, where the Palladium had brought the Greek city-states a hegemony of a thousand years. Scipio entered the mystery center beneath the Parthenon and carried forth the sacred image of Pallas Athena, bringing it to Rome and the temple of Vesta, where it stood as the guardian of the grandeur that was Rome. In the Civil War, Lincoln, the reincarnated Hamlet, led the tone of the Emancipators and accomplished a similar deed, giving the war to preserve the Union a moral dimension by making it a war to end slavery. Lincoln put the Emancipation Proclamation into effect on January 1, 1869. It was Lincoln's custom during the war years to read passages from *Hamlet* before going to sleep at night.

The first event of the falling action of *Hamlet* is a reversal of the final event of the rising action, in which Claudius sent spies to ferret out Hamlet's intentions. In the Act 3, Scene 3, Hamlet saw Claudius alone kneeling in prayer, yet he refused to take Claudius's life. This event demonstrated that the revenge demanded of Hamlet by the Ghost at the play's beginning was not simply a murder. This scene had appeared in *The Iliad* as an act of pure revenge. Achilles attacked the Trojan army, slaughtered their troops, and then slew Hector. Hector's death represented the reversal of his victories over the Greek army, the last event of the rising action in *The Iliad*. Homer's epic ends with the funeral of Hector, Tamer of Horses. Homer's other epic, Virgil's epic, and many plays of the tragedians tell more of the full tale of the Trojan War. In the American Civil War, General Meade's defeat of General Lee's army at Gettysburg is the event that corresponds to Achilles's victory over Hector and Hamlet's refusal to kill Claudius. It is a reversal of Lee's earlier victories. In a strange three days of battles in July of 1863, the reincarnated Priam (Robert E. Lee) threw away the flower of his troops by sending them against a dug-in enemy holding the high ground under the command of the reincarnated Agamemnon.

The second event of the falling action in *Hamlet* involved the death of Polonius at the hands of Hamlet. Polonius, hiding behind a tapestry and eavesdropping on the conversation between Gertrude and her son, is stabbed by Hamlet. He pays the price for plotting with Claudius, and in return Claudius receives certain knowledge of Hamlet's purpose. The corresponding event in the Trojan War involved the death of Achilles as he strutted back and forth in front of Troy and dared the Trojans to come out and fight. Paris's poisoned arrow struck him in his only weakness—the heal. Achilles's death unleashed a quarrel in the Greek army as devastating as the one that his argument with Agamemnon had caused earlier. A new leader had to be chosen but the choice of Odysseus seemed like a Pyrrhic victory. Ajax Telamon could not accept the army's verdict, fell into madness, and killed himself. In the

Civil War, the event corresponding to the election of a new military leader occurred on March 12, 1864. President Lincoln appointed U.S. Grant as the commander-in-chief of the Union armies. General Sherman replaced Grant as the commander of the Western armies. General Grant retained General Meade as the commander of the Army of the Potomac. The House of the Generals was then prepared to take on General Robert E. Lee. General Grant eschewed the tricks of an Odysseus, however, and simply wore down the remnant of Lee's forces. General Meade made sure every detail of his Commander's plan was carried out.

The final event of the falling action in *Hamlet* involved Prince Fortinbras's passage through Denmark on his way to attack Poland with the Norwegian army. This invasion was the culmination of the peace offering of Old Norway. Hamlet's journey to England took him in the opposite direction. It was the outcome of his visit to Ophelia and the nosiness of her father. King Claudius had a crafty plan to rid himself of Hamlet by sending him on this sea journey. The plan of the wily Odysseus to hide warriors in a wooden horse, a sacred offering to Athena—who was supposedly angry at Odysseus for his theft of her image, the Palladium—led to Troy burning to the ground. The culmination of the defeat of the Decapolis was thus accomplished a decade later. A similar culmination occurred in the Civil War. The fiasco of Bull Run led to Sherman's army conquering Atlanta. When General Sherman began his March to the Sea, his orders to burn certain supplies to prevent them from falling into Confederate hands resulted in the burning of Atlanta.

The second turning point in *Hamlet* occurred when Hamlet was on the high seas. After reading the commission that Claudius had sent the English king, Hamlet rewrote it and thus avoided being executed by the English king. The fire trial of his father's ghost and the command to revenge led to the water trial of his fight with pirates on the high seas and return to Denmark. In the Civil War, Lincoln willingly took the oath of the office of President. On January 31, 1865, the House of Representatives passed the bill that sent the thirteenth amendment of the Constitution to the states for its ratification. Its passage later that year enabled Lincoln to remove the blot upon the U.S. government caused by the enslavement of its people. He fulfilled his oath to uphold the Constitution by amending it.

The first event of the conclusion of *Hamlet* occurs in Act 5, Scene 1. Hamlet attends the funeral of Ophelia, a reversal of the corresponding event in the prologue—the marriage of his mother to his Uncle Claudius. In the Trojan War, a similar reversal occurred when Helen finally returned to Sparta to bring an end to the separation of the spirit of Greece, Apollo, from its homeland. The corresponding event in the Civil War was Lee's surrender to Grant at Appomattox. This event ended the war between the states. For the Confederacy it was a funeral; for the Union it was the return of Columbia, the spirit of America, to her homeland.

The last event in *Hamlet* is the duel between Laertes and Hamlet which results in the death of both combatants. It was an echo of the duel spoken of at the play's beginning, which pitted two kings in single combat to settle a dispute over land and to save two nations from a bloody war. The second duel was dishonorable and filled with lies—a cup steeped with poison, and a sword anointed with poison. The event ending the Trojan War also involved treachery as King Agamemnon was betrayed by his own wife, Clytemnestra. So too did the Civil War come to a conclusion with treachery—the assassination of President Lincoln. John Wilkes Booth thus added a third evil deed to his sacrilegious slaying of King Priam and his poisoning of King Hamlet and his son. The assassination of President Lincoln was also a reversal of the legal hanging of John Brown that had begun the Civil War.

The plot of Shakespeare's *Hamlet* can help bring clarity to two great wars—the Trojan War and the American Civil War. Although they are separated by three millennia, the famous figures involved and their world historic actions can be understood and judged fairly. When time is out of joint, some people arise to set it right, while others seek to perpetuate institutions that have outlived their time. More importantly, the ideas of reincarnation and destiny that stand behind the insights of the Bard reveal the racism of the white supremacist movement, which sought to maintain slavery in the United States, to be a complete lie and a fabrication. Frederick Douglass and Harriet Tubman, the Moses of her people, were great human beings. Their initiations in Troy in the thirteenth century B.C.

and in Elsinore in the ninth century should shine as beacons. We should look up to them and seek to emulate their example. Nor did they need any advantages to accomplish such deeds, but were self-educated, like Abraham Lincoln himself, and as devoted to their fellow man as few followers of the path of Christ could hope to achieve.

3.
George Washington and the Legend of Columbia

In the spring of 1998, I experienced an event that was very similar to the one eighteen years previously, when I had read a passage in a Steiner lecture stating that Hamlet was the reincarnation of Hector. In 1998 I was teaching a Shakespearean tragedy to high school seniors. Since I had used *Hamlet*, *Othello*, *Macbeth*, and *King Lear* in previous years of my world literature course, I decided instead to try *Antony and Cleopatra*. I had first studied it as a high school junior and then again in the Shakespeare course I had taken in college, and a third time in graduate school. What I didn't realize was how much my research on *Hamlet* and its relation to the death of Priam in *The Aeneid* had changed my worldview. In the third scene of act four in *Antony and Cleopatra*, Antony's soldiers hear a noise from under the earth. One of the soldiers explains its meaning by saying, "'Tis the god Hercules, whom Antony loved, now leaves him."

Shakespeare's source for most of his Roman plays was Plutarch. I reviewed Plutarch's biography of Antony and saw clear indications that Antony believed himself to be an ancestor of Hercules. Understanding Shakespeare's Hamlet as a reincarnation of Hector had led me to a scene in *The Aeneid* that reflected the possible earlier lives of five other characters in *Hamlet*. The legend of the Golden Fleece (also called "Jason and the Argonauts") was a staple of the freshman English course on Greek mythology and contained four other characters who seemed to be possible past lives of those famous Romans who founded the Roman Empire. I did not read the actual epic, *The Argonautica* by Apollonius of Rhodes, until later, but I had recently taught *Medea* by Euripides, which made insight into Cleopatra's previous incarnation easier to grasp. Rather then send another letter to the Anthroposophical Society leaders, I simply wrote out those events and the moral qualities that seemed to support the possibility of Antony being the reincarnation of Hercules, of Cleopatra being Medea, Octavius being Jason, Julius Caesar being Aegeus, and Marcus Brutus being Theseus. When I typed it up, "Hercules in Roman History" was fourteen pages in length. The main difference between the letter to Hiebel and this article/outline was that the former involved one Shakespeare play—*Hamlet*—but the latter included two—*Julius Caesar* and *Antony and Cleopatra*.

The circle of the founders of the Roman empire seemed to be the reincarnation of the circle of those who had founded ancient Greece. The great heroes of Greek myths were led by Heracles and were called the first generation of heroes. Achilles was the leader of the second generation of heroes, who gained their fame through their victory in the Trojan War. My assumption that the great heroes of Greece—Hercules, Theseus, Jason, and Orpheus—reincarnated as the founders of the Roman Empire was only tentative. It did make the work easier, since I was focusing on the Argonauts shifting one zodiacal sign clockwise in their Roman incarnation. Plutarch's *Lives* also proved helpful since he had written biographies of six of the members of the circle of the founders of the Roman Empire. His biographies of Cicero and Pompey pointed to their possible earlier lives as Orpheus and Aeëtes, the king of Colchis. With the addition of Cassius, who would have been the reincarnated Pirithous, eight members of the Roman circle would have had an earlier incarnation in ancient Greece or in Colchis.

Charts E and F present the current status of my research into the first generation of Greek heroes. The idea that the advancement of a hero (or his initiation) results in his skipping over a sign, but also causes the one skipped over to be retained in the same sign for another incarnation was discussed in chapter two. Another example of this phenomenon apparently occurred with Orpheus's initiation, which forced Aeëtes to remain in the tone of intuitionism and become a member of the House of the Emperors. The idea that a member of a circle may leave it and a substitute, as it were, would be found to take his or her place was discussed in chapter one. The appearance of Lepidus in the position that the reincarnated Phrixus would have taken is such a case. The role of Phrixus at the very beginning of the legend of the Golden Fleece is similar to that of Helen at the onset of the Trojan War. Helen is the bearer of the spirit of Greece—the god Apollo, to use the mythological language—who will guide the city-states through his oracle at Delphi. When Phrixus arrived in Aeëtes's kingdom, he sacrificed the winged ram that had saved him and his sister from the

CHART E

The Circle of the Great Heroes of Ancient Greece and Their Three Houses (or Tones)

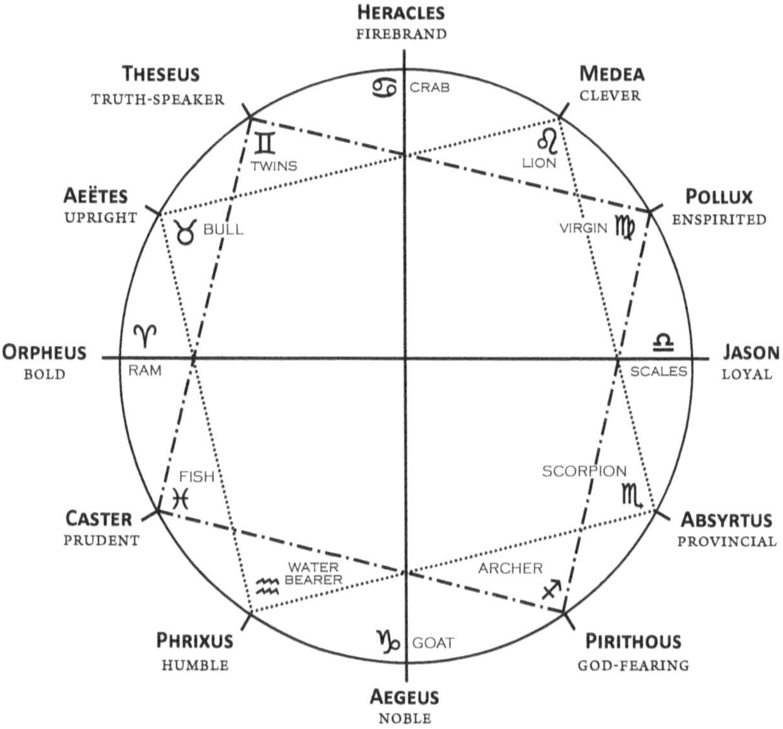

HERACLES — FIREBRAND (♋ CRAB)
THESEUS — TRUTH-SPEAKER (♊ TWINS)
MEDEA — CLEVER (♌ LION)
AEËTES — UPRIGHT (♉ BULL)
POLLUX — ENSPIRITED (♍ VIRGIN)
ORPHEUS — BOLD (♈ RAM)
JASON — LOYAL (♎ SCALES)
CASTER — PRUDENT (♓ FISH)
ABSYRTUS — PROVINCIAL (♏ SCORPION)
PHRIXUS — HUMBLE (♒ WATER BEARER)
PIRITHOUS — GOD-FEARING (♐ ARCHER)
AEGEUS — NOBLE (♑ GOAT)

	HOUSE OF ATHENS & SPARTA *theism - sun* ☉	HOUSE OF COLCHIS *intuitionism - moon* ☾	ARGONAUTS *naturalism - earth* ⊕
NORTH	THESEUS	MEDEA	HERACLES
EAST	POLLUX	ABSYRTUS	JASON
SOUTH	PIRITHOUS	PHRIXUS	AEGEUS
WEST	CASTER	AEËTES	ORPHEUS

CHART F

The Circle of the Founders of the Roman Empire and Their Three Houses (or Tones)

BRUTUS — CRAB ♋
CICERO — TWINS ♊
ANTONY — LION ♌
POMPEY — BULL ♉
CLEOPATRA — VIRGIN ♍
CAEPIO CATO — RAM ♈
CATO THE YOUNGER — SCALES ♎
(LEPIDUS) — FISH ♓
OCTAVIUS — SCORPION ♏
JULIUS CAESAR — WATER BEARER ♒
POMPEY'S SON — ARCHER ♐
CASSIUS — GOAT ♑

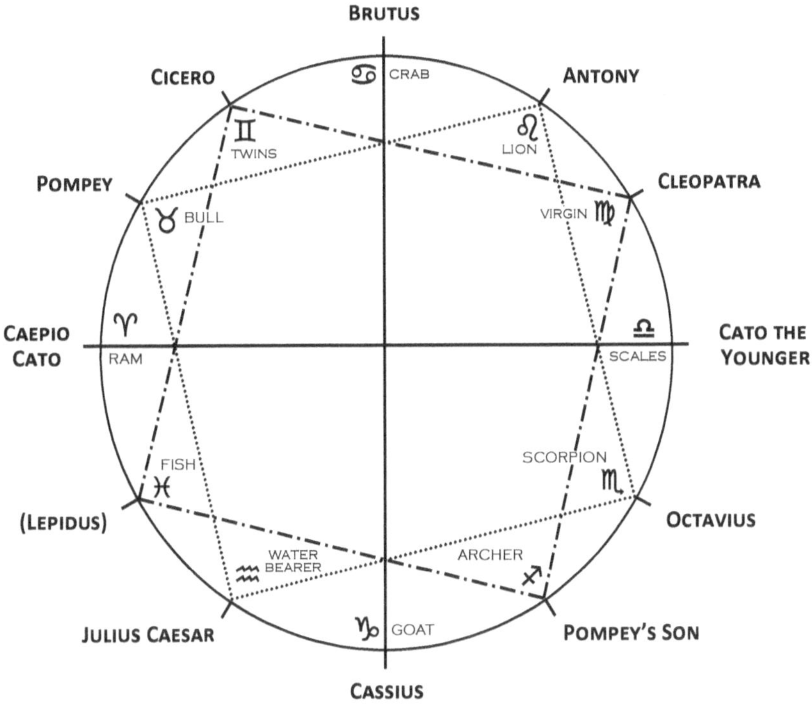

		SENATORS *theism - thinking* ☉	EMPERORS *intuitionism - feeling* ☾	CONSPIRATORS *naturalism - willing* ⊕
NORTH	←	CICERO*	ANTONY*	BRUTUS*
EAST	←	CLEOPATRA	OCTAVIUS	CATO THE YOUNGER*
SOUTH	←	POMPEY'S SON	CAESAR*	CASSIUS
WEST	←	(LEPIDUS)	POMPEY*	CAEPIO CATO

evil queen. Phrixus gave the coat of the ram—the Golden Fleece—to the king of Colchis as a gift. The Golden Fleece is the symbol of Apollo's power to foresee the future. The reason that the fifty great heroes assembled at the foot of Mount Pelion was to bring the glory of Apollo's rulership back to Greece.

The next step in the research on the first generation of Greek heroes followed logically from the research on the second generation. If the second generation had had the mission of defending the Greeks, the Romans, and then the English from the decadence of the Eastern, the Southern, and the Northern mystery streams, the first generation, the founders of Greece and then Rome, would probably go next to England. A work of English literature does exist which tells of such a deed, though it is the sole epic that survived the destruction of the Anglo-Saxon culture that the Catholic Church visited upon England following William the Conqueror's victory in 1066.

English literature teachers often skip *Beowulf* altogether or present it in the same fashion that they use for Greeks mythology—as a children's fable. Consequently, even literate adults tend to remember little about the story except Beowulf killing the monster Grendel. One of three houses in *Beowulf*—the House of the Danes—is made up of the conspirators from ancient Rome. Hrothgar and Unferth are reincarnations of Brutus and Cassius, while Esher and Wulfgar are the reborn Cato the Younger and Caepio Cato. Another tone—that of theism (thinking)—is composed of the emperors and can be called the House of the Swedes. It includes Onela (Pompey),

Edgetho (Antony), and Hathcyn (Caesar), but the fourth member—Ongentho (Pompey's son)—remained in the same sign of Sagitarius without advancing. Higlac (Octavian) skipped over him, as it were, since he had entered a mystery center in Rome and had received initiation there. Strange it is that Plutarch did not write a biography of this most famous of all the Romans, but the prohibition against revealing the mystery center's secrets probably demanded that he not do so.[7]

The house of the Geats is the tone of naturalism or willing. It includes two members who had been initiated—Herbald (Cicero) and Higlac (Octavian)—and the sole remaining member of the house of Colchis, Thrith (Cleopatra). The fourth member, the mighty Beowulf, had been in the house of Colchis, but only because of his gift to the king. Phrixus had had Lepidus replace him during the time of the Roman Empire. The hours that Beowulf swam submerged in the great ocean referred not to the waters of the Baltic Sea, but to the astral world, the world of imagination. This world is usually experienced when dreaming, though Beowulf could wake up in his dreams, as it were. The monster he fought was the spirit of civil strife, the same that Antony had unleashed when he summoned the spirits of Julius Caesar and of Discord at the end of Act 3, Scene 1. To clarify this idea, the bard of *Beowulf* describes how Beowulf undertook an even greater task after he defeated Grendel. He journeyed to the Underworld to fight Grendel's mother, whom the bard identified as the She-wolf of Rome.

---

[7] Octavius's initiation might also explain why he demanded that *The Aeneid* not be burned per Virgil's request. His desire to make public the truth of reincarnation may have moved him.

Previously, I discussed an insight that occurred on November 24, 1998 that connected Aeneas's escape from Troy with Douglass's escape from slavery in the South. My research on the past lives of the circle of twelve characters in *Hamlet* led to insights into the circle of the leaders of the American Civil War. Two separate lines of research came together. My personal interest in *Hamlet* and *The Aeneid* had seized on Steiner's comment in a lecture on the Gospel of St. Mark and developed into a series of three later incarnations of a group of twelve world historic leaders. My research on spiritual groups in America (like Edgar Cayce's Association for Research and Enlightenment) and spiritual impulses in this country (like Baum's *Wizard of Oz*) was conducted in an interest group of the Rudolf Steiner Branch in Chicago. I felt that I had to decide between my personal research, begun in 1980, and the American research I had taken up in 1985. After carefully assembling all of my research folders, I concluded that I should pursue the research of the interest group, when a picture arose in my mind about the visit of Phillis Wheatley to General Washington in Cambridge, Massachusetts during the American Revolution. I assumed that Washington would have asked her to read the poem she had written, but as I began to imagine her reading it, another picture interposed itself—that of Cleopatra before Antony's dead body and her inability to tell him, while alive, of her love for him and her belief in his greatness. In a different life she was perhaps granted the chance to do so.

As I began to see the past lives of Jefferson and others, the question arose of whether this insight into Washington and the Founding Fathers might also help deepen my understanding of the Civil War. The picture of Douglass's escape from slavery then arose, and I was hard at work the following day writing down the two full circles of Founding Fathers and Civil War leaders. *The Sanctuary for the Rights of Mankind* focused on the elements of destiny that surrounded the meeting of Washington and Wheatley. The House of the Generals (that is, the tone of naturalism or willing) includes two individuals who were held back. Neither Aaron Burr nor Benedict Arnold would follow Washington's orders, and Arnold even committed treason. Their replacements, Lafayette and von Steuben, both did an admirable job. The House of the Presidents had returned to the same tone of theism or thinking that its four members had worked out of during the founding of Ancient Greece. The House of the Writers contained the new members from the time when it was the House of Colchis—the foremost orator, Patrick Henry, and the most stirring essayist, Thomas Paine. An attempt was made in *A Sanctuary for the Rights of Mankind* to suggest how extraordinary the life of Benjamin Franklin actually was. Chart G attempts to clarify the tones and worldviews of the Founding Fathers.

The plots of the world historic events that founded Ancient Greece, the Roman Empire, and the United States of America are as complex and interwoven as the lives of the great men and women who took part in them. Just as the plot

CHART G

The Circle of the Founding Fathers of the United States of America and Their Three Houses

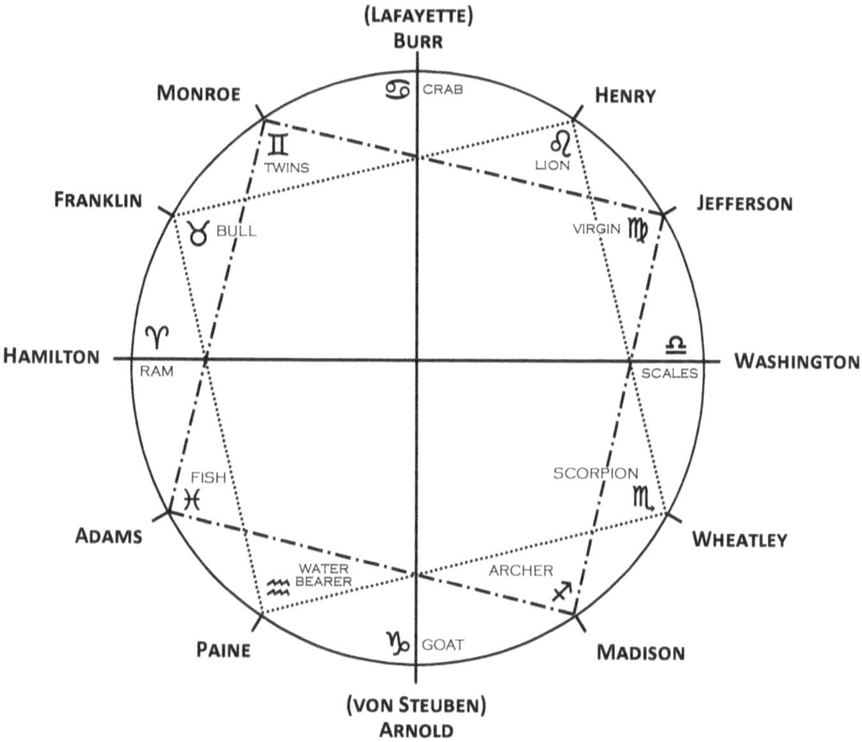

	PRESIDENTS	WRITERS	GENERALS
	theism	*intuitionism*	*naturalism*
	☉	☾	⊕
NORTH	JAMES MONROE	PATRICK HENRY	AARON BURR
EAST	THOMAS JEFFERSON	PHILLIS WHEATLEY	GEORGE WASHINGTON
SOUTH	JAMES MADISON	THOMAS PAINE	BENEDICT ARNOLD
WEST	JOHN ADAMS	BEN FRANKLIN	ALEXANDER HAMILTON

of the Civil War can be grasped more fully and deeply by comparing it to the plot of *Hamlet* and *The Illiad*, so the plot of America's founding can be understood more fully by comparing it to the plots of *Julius Caesar* and *Antony and Cleopatra* as well as *The Argonautica* and legend of Theseus. The first event of the founding of the Roman empire occurred in Asia, where Pompey had travelled with his army after ridding the Mediterranean Sea of the danger of piracy. He sought to capture or destroy the army of Mithridates, but a series of miraculous escapes made that impossible. When he did return to Rome in 66 B.C., Pompey's triumphal procession outdid any previous victories of Roman generals or any that would later occur. He had expanded the empire to include sixteen nations of Asia, including the easternmost country of Colchis. Through Pompey's exploits, Mars, the guardian spirit of Rome, now ruled over most of the known world. Pompey also ended piracy and brought more tributes to Rome than had been brought by all its previous victors. In the *Argonautica*, the escape of Phrixus on the winged ram is equally a miracle, while Phrixus's gift to King Aeëtes (the past life of Pompey) is precious beyond all monetary value—the Golden Fleece. The prologue to the founding of the United States of America similarly begins with three close escapes from death by George Washington and the gift of the Albany Plan in 1754 by the reincarnated Phrixus.[8]

The next stage in the development of the Roman Empire involved events surrounding the emergence of the first tri-

---

[8] See chapters 2 and 3 of *A Sanctuary for the Rights of Mankind*, Rick Spaulding and Maurice York, Wrightwood Press, Chicago, 2008.

umvirate. It can be compared to the tests that King Aeëtes required of Jason in order to recover the Golden Fleece and return it to Greece. In America, these tests appeared in the form of the abuses of King George III. The protests against the Stamp Act in 1765, as well as the demonstrations over other acts of Parliament inspired by orators like Patrick Henry and James Otis, helped to unify the thirteen colonies. These events in American history appeared in Roman history as Caesar arranging his daughter's marriage to Pompey. In the *Argonautica*, King Aeëtes laid the task of yoking the fire-breathing bulls upon Jason. Jason's second task from King Aeëtes was to sow the dragon's teeth into the earth. In Roman history this trial appeared as the formation of the first triumvirate, which joined Julius Caesar and Pompey together as rulers over the Roman government. In the the time of the Founding Fathers, the corresponding event appeared as the emergence of the First Continental Congress in 1774, which challenged British power over the colonies in America. The armed intervention of King George III began with closing the port of Boston. The war itself began on April 18, 1775 with the Battle of Concord. On May 10, 1775, George Washington was appointed Commander-in-chief and incorporated the Minutemen into the Continental Army. The following year on July 4th, the Declaration of Independence was read aloud in Philadelphia, and Columbia stepped forth onto the stage of world history. What Jason had done in retrieving the Golden Fleece of Apollo and returning the folk soul of Greece to his oracle at Delphi, and what Julius Caesar had accomplished by winning the Gaelic wars to extend the rulership of Mars and the folk soul of Rome over Europe, Washington was to achieve in America as Columbia's champion. While Jason had the aid of Medea to give him victory, Caesar—according to Plutarch—somehow possessed something like Medea's magic that inhered in his very name. Plutarch observed that the power of the name of Caesar brought him victories. Following the death of Crassus and the ending of the first triumvirate, Caesar quickly gained hegemony in Italy, while Pompey fled to Asia.

The first turning point in the Columbian legend occurred during the aftermath of the British Army's first resounding victory, the Battle of Long Island. With the help of Alexander Hamilton, Washington's army of 4,000 was able to escape capture by General Howe's army of 8,000 soldiers by crossing over the Delaware River. On Christmas Eve of 1776, Washington launched a ten-day campaign, one of the most brilliant attacks in military history, by crossing back over the river, capturing the Hessian mercenaries and their supplies in Trenton, and outfoxing the British Redcoats who had come to the aid of their allies. The American people took heart, and the King of France decided to send an army to America's aid and put it under Washington's command.

A similar turning point occurred in the *Argonautica* when Jason left his teacher Chiron and went to challenge Pelias in order to recover his kingdom. Jason came to a river where he met an old woman who asked him for help to carry her across to the other side. He agreed and lifted her up, but when he stepped into the water, she suddenly became heavier. He used all of his strength to complete the task, losing a sandal in the mud in the process. After the completion of this task Jason showed Hera (for she only appeared to be an old woman) that he was ready for his adventure. The turning point in the founding of the Roman Empire also took place before a river. Roman generals were not allowed to bring their troops into Italy proper, bounded by the Rubicon river. When Caesar returned from Gaul (France) to oppose Pompey, he had to decide whether to do so politically, or to instigate a civil war. His decision for war ("the die is cast") signaled the end of the period of the Roman Republic.

The rising action of the Columbian legend occurred during the Revolutionary War. In 1777, General Burgoyne brought his army down from Canada. The British strategy was to have General Howe's army advance up the Hudson River, meet Burgoyne's army at Albany, and thus separate the Continental Army from New England. General Howe failed to receive his orders and decided instead to travel up the Delaware River to capture the American capital, Philadelphia. Howe persisted with this plan even after discovering his orders to meet General Burgoyne as part of the British divide-and-conquer strategy. Burgoyne's defeat in the Battle of Saratoga led to the French entering the war, tipping the scales that Wheatley had envisioned in her poem to General Washington unalterably in favor of Columbia. The Battle of Saratoga can be compared to Caesar's Italian campaign and Pompey's flight to Asia. It may also be compared to the escape of the Argonauts from Colchis with the aid of Medea.

General Washington defeated General Cornwallis in 1781 at the Battle of Yorktown. Washington's capture of the British army sealed the victory of Columbia. Like the defeat of the giant Talus by the Argonauts on their return from Colchis, a seemingly invincible giant—the British Redcoats—was laid low. Washington's triumph can also be compared to Julius Caesar's victory over Pompey's army at the Battle of Pharsalia. The Treaty of Paris in 1783 brought the Revolutionary War to its conclusion, making the defeat of King George III an historical fact. The death of Pompey in Egypt accomplished a similar deed for Pompey's army. The return of Jason to Greece with the Golden Fleece likewise showed his right to the rulership of his kingdom, while the death of Pelias gave it to him beyond all question.

The high point or climax of the Columbian legend occurred in Philadelphia. After four more years under the Articles of Confederation, the Founding Fathers decided to join together again in 1787 to form a new constitution. Washington was unanimously elected president of the Constitutional Convention, and thirty-nine delegates from the various states signed their names to the Constitution, which was then ratified by the states. James Madison was its author—the Father of the Constitution. Like Argus who built the *Argo*, the ship that carried the fifty Greek heroes who sought to recover the Golden Fleece, Madison constructed the American ship-of-state. His effort to join the Roman idea of the republic with the Greek ideal of democracy can also be seen as a rejection of the idea of kingship that motivated Julius Caesar and led to the founding of the Roman Empire. Just as Cato the Younger joined with Brutus to oppose Caesar, so did Madison unite with Jefferson to defeat Hamilton's idea of continuing the British form of monarchy in the New World. Hamilton ended up supporting the Constitution by writing essays for the *Federalist Papers*, but the pseudonym he used for his essays was Julius Caesar.

The events during Washington's two terms as President along with those during John Adams's term can be compared to the voyage of the Argonauts on their journey to Colchis, as well as the events involving the second triumvirate in Rome, which were presented by Shakespeare in *Antony and Cleopatra*. A similar comparison could be made between the events of Jefferson's presidency and the myth of Theseus, as well as the events in *Julius Caesar*. Chart H summarizes these comparisons.

In order to understand the Founding Fathers' idea of the Temple of Liberty it needs to be placed in the context of Freemasonry. Over a thirty-three-year period, Benjamin Franklin crafted the Albany Plan and the Articles of Confederation and then worked closely with both Jefferson and Madison to formulate the Declaration of Independence and the United States Constitution. Whereas Rudolf Steiner created a foundation stone to provide a path of initiation for free human beings to gain access to the spiritual world, Franklin and the Founding Fathers created a foundation stone that provided a new form of government for free human beings to live together in a Blessed Community. They called the spiritual realm where Columbia could reside and inspire her followers the Temple of Liberty. For Thomas Jefferson, the possibility of bringing this high ideal into the earthy realm was of special importance. He envisioned how the six principles of the Constitution could reappear outwardly in the architecture of the Capitol Building.

If a foundation stone presents a pathway to a form of government suitable for free human beings, and a building provides a conduit for the spiritual activity of the Founders, the next stage would be to have a new generation take up their missions. This generation of Civil War leaders had to "provide new pillars of the temple of liberty formed of pure thought, and molded into general intelligence, sound morality, and in particular, a reverence for the constitution and laws," as Abraham Lincoln suggested in a speech to commemorate the fiftieth anniversary of the ratification of the Constitution This second generation of Americans accomplished, not just a world historic victory on the battlefield, but a transformation of their soul-spiritual organisms and a feat of self-development that the Founders referred to with the term "apotheosis."

A group of artists, architects, and sculptors gathered around Daniel Burnham to honor Columbia in 1893 with the Columbian Exposition in Chicago, which began the City Beautiful Movement. In 1915, they were chosen to honor her again in the city dedicated to her—Washington, the District of Columbia. They took the ideas of the Founders and developed them further by expanding the Washington Mall and constructing the Lincoln Memorial as a counterpart to the Capitol Building, and the Jefferson Memorial as counterpart to the White House. The three pillars of Freemasonry—wisdom,

CHART H

The Columbian Legend
(1788 - 1826)

(Apollo)	(Mars)	(Columbia)
FOUNDING OF GREECE	FOUNDING OF THE ROMAN EMPIRE	FOUNDING OF THE UNITED STATES
Voyage of the Argo	*Antony and Cleopatra*	*The Federalists*
1. Women of Lemnos tempt Argonauts to stay with them	1. Antony with Cleopatra in Egypt	1. Unanimous vote for Pres. Washington (honeymoon)
2. Samothrace mysteries	2. Soothsayer warns Antony to avoid Octavius	2. Franklin's petition to end slavery
3. King Cyzicus is accidentaly killed	3. Sertius Pompey is murdered	3. Hamilton and Madison make deal to build the U.S. Capitol
4. Jason defeats Heracles in a rowing contest	4. Octavius defeats Antony in sea battle at Actium	4. Washington retires after two terms
5. Polydeuces wins boxing contest	5. Octavius defeats Antony's army and drives to Alexandria	5. John Adams runs for President
6. King Phineas is freed from the harpies	6. Antony commits suicide	6. Washington's "Farewell Address"
7. The dove is used to pass the clashing rocks	7. *Pax Romana*	7. Adams makes peace treaty with France

CHART H (cont.)

The Columbian Legend
(1788 - 1826)

(Apollo) FOUNDING OF GREECE	(Mars) FOUNDING OF THE ROMAN EMPIRE	(Columbia) FOUNDING OF THE UNITED STATES
Myth of Theseus	*Julius Caesar*	The Democrats
1. Theseus defeats the Minotaur	1. Brutus rejects Caesar's idea of kingship	1. Jefferson wins disputed election of 1800
2. Ariadne helps Theseus, but he abandons her	2. Cassius forms a conspiracy against Caesar	2. Jefferson agrees to Louisiana Purchase in 1803
3. Theseus neglects to change black sails and Aegeus dies	3. Brutus and Cassius kill Caesar in the Roman Senate	3. Burr kills Hamilton in a duel
4. Theseus brings democracy to Athens	4. Brutus offers freedom to Romans	4. Jefferson "republican- izes" government
5. Theseus befriends Pirithous	5. The conspirators flee Athens	5. Jefferson and Adams resume correspondence
6. The friends kidnap Helen, but her brothers bring her home	6. Brutus and Cassius fight against second triumvirate	6. War of 1812 (Second Revolution- ary War)
7. Theseus and Pirithous try to kidnap Persephone, but Hades defeats them	7. The conspirators both die at Philippi	7. Jefferson and Adams both die on July 4, 1826 (50th anniversary of signing)

beauty, and strength—are embodied in the cultures of Egypt, Greece, and Rome. The Washington Monument, an Egyptian obelisk, was completed in the nineteenth century. Burnham's architects, Bacon and Pope, took the Parthenon and the Pantheon as models to commemorate their memorials to the generations of the Civil War and of the Founding Fathers. What the Founding Fathers had themselves fought and died for, and what the following generation sought to preserve and defend against the onslaughts of decadence and injustice, were now united. The Temple of Liberty was not built in a day. Its genesis can be found in ancient Egyptian times when the Argonauts set sail to renew the temple of Apollo and the suitors of Helen left for Troy to recover the spirit of Greece.

4.
Mahatma Gandhi and the Independence of India

Gandhi began writing his autobiography in 1925 at the age of fifty-six. He wrote a chapter each week, which appeared in *Navajivan*, one of his two weekly journals. Its one-hundred-and-sixty-seven chapters were eventually published in book form—volume one in 1927 and volume two in 1929. Gandhi divided its contents into five parts. Part one contains twenty-five chapters and tells of his birth on October 2, 1869 in Porbandar, India. It then examines his childhood and youth up to the age of twenty-one.

Gandhi identified his foremost moral quality with the words "I never lied." He provided numerous examples of this virtue, which he shared in common with "Honest Abe" Lincoln and George (I cannot tell a lie) Washington. Gandhi even titled his autobiography *The Story of My Experiments with Truth*. He concluded his life's story with a "Farewell" in which he extolled Truth: "My uniform experience has convinced me that there is no other God than Truth.... The little fleeting glimpses, therefore, that I have been able to have of Truth can hardly convey an idea of the indescribable luster of Truth, a million times more intense that that of the sun we daily see with our eyes.... To see the universal and all-pervading Spirit of Truth face to face one must be able to love the meanest of creation as oneself."

Gandhi named other personal qualities in his attempt to characterize his youthful self. He said that he was very shy, respectful, and obedient, but he did not present these qualities as virtues. His inability to speak in public lasted into his adulthood even as his early obedience to authority gradually matured into civil disobedience. He identified naive trust in others as the vice that beset him. His friends warned him that one of his closest confidants was actually a con man. Unfortunately, he had to experience such crises in his young adulthood before he learned the lesson that his own good qualities were not sufficiently strong to miraculously transform the people he befriended.

He accepted the Hindu tradition that allowed his parents to arrange his marriage and that assigned an inferior position to women and entered an arranged marriage at the age of thirteen. He tried to force his child bride, Kasturbai, to conform to the ideal of the ignorant, submissive wife. Years went by before the idea of woman's equality dawned on him. Fortunately for Kasturbai, Hindu tradition allowed her to escape back to her parents' home for six months during each of her teenage years.

In 1887 Gandhi travelled to England to study law in London. He was required to "keep terms," that is, to attend six formal dinners and to pass exams on Roman law and English common law. He played the role of both the English gentleman and the bachelor. Despite his seemingly lavish lifestyle, Gandhi was actually very frugal, but this double life of false pretenses did not suit him. He ended it by writing a letter to the young lady whom he was seeing to inform her of his already-married state. The admission of the truth helped, and he became her good friend.

While in London, Gandhi met Madame Blavatsky and Annie Besant, the leaders of the Theosophical Society. He was aware that Theosophists tended to use their friends, especially if they were Hindu, for political purposes. He viewed his experiences with the Theosophical Society as a benefit, however, and began reading the *Bhagavad Gita* due to their influence. The "Song of the Blessed One" later helped Gandhi overcome his doubts about religion, which arose at this time in his life. In 1901 he visited Besant when she was in India. Later in 1920 he sought her support for his policy of noncooperation with England.

When he returned from England at age twenty-one, Gandhi met a man who was four years his senior, Raychandbhai, whose passion was self-realization: "to see God in every one of my daily acts."[9] Gandhi felt that Raychandbhai was his spirit guide, a religious leader greater than any other. Though he did not look upon him as a guru to be blindly followed, Raychandbhai did help Gandhi with his effort to study the Koran and other religions and to find the unifying thread that brought them into harmony. Raychandbhai's influence on Gandhi was similar to a book by Tolstoy, which he read in 1893. *The Kingdom of God Is Within You* moved him deeply and changed the way he viewed himself.

---

9 *The Story of My Experiments with Truth*, Mohandas K. Gandhi. Boston, Beacon Press, 1957, p.88.

By profession, Gandhi was a lawyer. His first job required him to move to South Africa in 1893, to the city of Durban in the colony of Natal, where the company that he was representing was being sued. By finding a compromise to the lawsuit brought against his client, an Indian merchant named Abdulla, Gandhi found a way to overcome a mistaken tradition of the legal profession. Rather than engaging in endless litigation, Gandhi helped negotiate a settlement—the true purpose of civil law. He began the fight against a second tradition by making an unexpected decision at the farewell dinner held in his honor. Rather than accept the success and depart, Gandhi decided to remain in South Africa and oppose a bill that denied Indians their right to vote in the providence of Natal. He began the fight against the tradition of dehumanizing Indians and marginalizing them as "coolies." He began circulating petitions, and in 1894 founded the Natal Indian Congress (NIC).

By working as a lawyer in South Africa and preparing Abdulla's case, Gandhi had to forego any attempt to remedy the mistreatment of Indians in his homeland. He had experienced such abuse himself when railroad employees insulted him and made him ride in the third-class compartment for Indians. Yet as a result of the British importing forced laborers to their plantations in South Africa, Durban was home to the largest population of Indians outside of India. This double life was not as filled with pretense as when he played the gentlemen in England. After founding the NIC, however, he determined that even with his new responsibilities he could take up the cause of helping indentured servants there in Durban, who were suffering even worse injustice than the "coolies."

One of the greatest challenges for a group like the Natal Indian Congress is the need to raise money. Gandhi realized that depending on wealthy donors who would bring in the necessary funds would be an undesirable substitute for engaging the oppressed in their own awakening.[10] Using common sense, he created a reasonable dues structure for becoming a member of NIC. Well-to-do people could pay more for membership than others. The frugality of Gandhi's cadre, coupled with his own down-to-earth practicality, was decisive in helping the fledgling social movement to secure a degree of financial stability.

In the summer of 1896, Gandhi returned to India in order to bring his wife and children back to South Africa to live with him. The storm at sea on their return voyage prefigured the storm of hatred that greeted them when they arrived in Durban. Gandhi needed his family with him so that they too could help to serve the community. The lack of this ideal of service in the public schools required that Gandhi provide home schooling for his children. Gandhi viewed service to the community as the basis of self-realization. His heart's desire was to serve the poor. Taking on the case of Balasundaram, an indentured servant unjustly beaten by his master who sought his assistance, led him to defend the many other indentured servants who began flocking to him.

---

10 The present-day equivalent of such wealthy donors would include not-for-profit foundations

Gandhi continued his study of the history of religion and began to read the *Upanishads*. When he returned to India in 1900, he stayed with Gokhale, one of the foremost Indian leaders of Congress. He tried to visit two of the finest spiritual leaders in India, the Maharishi Tagore and Vivekananda, but they were unable to meet with him. The latter had become famous for bringing Hinduism to the West and helping to form the Parliament of World Religions in 1893 at the Columbian World's Exposition in Chicago.

Gandhi began to realize that Indians in South Africa were suffering a fate like that of the Jews in Europe or the Untouchables in India. They lived in ghettoes and were shunned as "coolies." In 1903 the unsanitary conditions of their community in the slums of Johannesburg led to an outbreak of the bubonic plague. Gandhi and a few helpers guided their evacuation to a location thirteen miles away from the city. He then took on their legal cases, and they called him brother. He assisted them in building a tent city and depositing what money they had in a bank.

Gandhi credited his religious tolerance to the influence of his father's friends. He had close friendships with many white people and with members of various religions. Some biographers have questioned whether his tolerance extended to black people. Gandhi's actions speak to his viewpoint. In the Boer War of 1899—in which the British Empire engaged in battle against two South African states that rose up to oppose their rule—the British troops, due to their prejudice, refused to aid the injured Zulu warriors. Gandhi formed an ambulance corps to care for the wounded and willingly helped nurse them back to health.

Gandhi renewed his study of the *Bhagavad Gita* in 1903. In the following year, at age thirty-five, he began to use it for his morning meditation. For about thirty minutes he memorized verses and reviewed those verses that he had already learned by heart. He completely memorized thirteen chapters of the *Gita*. Gradually it dawned on him that this sacred book had become his dictionary for understanding the people whom he had met, as well as the deeper meaning of the events that occurred in his daily life. This morning meditation gradually led to the realization that his family included all of mankind. It also helped him to form the principle of Satyagraha in 1906.

Gandhi launched a weekly journal, *Indian Opinion*, in 1904, the same year that he read John Ruskin's *Unto This Last*. Gandhi was deeply moved by Ruskin's work and considered it to be as important for his spiritual development as Tolstoy's *The Kingdom of God is Within You*. He translated it as *The Welfare of All* and considered it the basis for his development of Satyagraha. He had earlier in his life experienced an inner voice, but now he had to give voice to his higher self. His articles became the vehicle for Satyagraha to take root in the Indian community in Natal. He wrote essays and articles until he left South Africa in 1915. They educated his readers about the facts surrounding various social issues and inspired them to take up the struggle against injustice. Led by Albert West, his co-workers carried *Indian Opinion* despite all of the difficulties involved. They continued to publish it even after Gandhi returned to India.

The Phoenix settlement became composed of many families who helped with the publication of *Indian Opinion*. Each family lived on a small monthly allowance from the income generated by the farm. Running the press was work they did in their spare time. Everyone learned typesetting. The families built houses out of corrugated steel on one of the five-acre plots belonging to the settlement. Self-reliance, frugality, and service to the community allowed the Phoenix settlement to succeed.

Gandhi founded the Tolstoy Farm, his second ashram, in 1912, two years after its namesake's death. It was a further development of the Phoenix settlement, dedicated not to publishing *Indian Opinion*, but to the spiritual improvement of its members. Hindu, Parsi, Muslim, and Christian families worked together and practiced Satyagraha. Gandhi became headmaster for the children at Tolstoy Farm and further developed his pedagogical ideas.[11] He fostered religious unity by having the children take part in communal fasting for Ramadan. He also had them participate in gardening, shoemaking, and carpentry. He developed their minds culturally by teaching literature and religion and refused to use corporal punishment, encouraging the better students to help those who misbehaved. He always blamed himself for such misbehavior in the children and even went on a fast when he thought it necessary.

Many of Gandhi's co-workers in South Africa travelled to India when he returned there in 1915. Gandhi founded the

---

11 Ibid. pp. 328-333.

Satyagraha Ashram to express outwardly its inner mission of practicing Satyagraha and creating a life of simplicity for its twenty-five members. When an untouchable family asked to join the ashram, Gandhi received approval for their entrance from his co-workers. He saw the addition of an untouchable family to the ashram as an attempt to bring Hinduism into the modern age.

Gandhi's mission had expanded from service to the community to freeing a country from the chains of imperialism. The goal of independence for India required uniting with Muslims and helping them to solve the Caliphate question. A deepening of Gandhi's meditative work was also necessary. The vow of silence on political issues, which Gandhi had received from Gokhale in 1915, became the practice of silence on Mondays. The eightfold path of Gautama Buddha designated Mondays as an opportunity to attain Right Word—speaking thoughtfully and avoiding gossip. Gandhi used Mondays to think through his ideas about hand-spinning and other initiatives that he was planning. In inner quiet, he carefully considered their effect on peasant life, on Indian society as a whole, and on world trade—especially how such a change could improve the quality of life and how to mitigate possible unintended consequences.

The Kheda Satyagraha, a protest organized by Gandhi in 1918, led to wide-spread repression. Gandhi admitted the error of not training his followers to have reverence for the law and the way of nonviolent protest. Gandhi's cadres undertook to correct his "Himalayan miscalculation" by creating workshops and other forums to educate people who would participate in such protests. These classes and workshops on nonviolent civil disobedience were a forerunner for those later led by American protest groups such as the Student Nonviolent Coordinating Committee (SNCC) and Southern Christian Leadership Center (SCLC). The increase in police oppression and arbitrary arrests in the Kheda district resulted in two weeklies, *Young India* and *Navajivan*, being offered to Gandhi for his use. Gandhi's writing attained an even higher stage of development as the inspiration of the Spirit of Truth began to open a pathway for Satyagraha to enter Indian society as a whole.

Gandhi's arrest and trial in 1922 became an historic phenomenon. Gandhi had finally overcome his shyness, and the world press took note of the Spirit of Truth present in his words to the presiding judge. While in prison afterwards, he began to write his autobiography, itself an "experiment with truth." The pages Gandhi wrote contain the pathway to the world of Providence wherein the revelation of God as the spirit of Truth can be found.

When Gandhi was granted an early release from prison in 1924, he sought to lift up the living standard of hundreds of millions of villagers in India and formed the Spinners Association. He located the Satyagraha Ashram in Ahmedabad, which had been an ancient center of handloom weaving, in part because he felt that the cottage industry of hand-spinning that he envisioned would have a suitable field for revival there. Almost a decade would have to pass before an understanding of how to achieve this revival in practical manner could finally emerge.

Gandhi withdrew from councils and stayed aloof from politics, refusing to take part in the constitutional reform conference of 1927. He denounced British imperialism and its divide-and-conquer strategy, which used reforms only to preserve control and drive wedges between different religions as well as between social classes to pit them against each other.

Gandhi campaigned against the unjust British salt tax in 1930. His protest involved marching two-hundred-and-forty miles to the Indian Ocean, picking up lumps of salt at the seashore, and bringing them back to their inland villages. Thousands of Indians emulated his example, and many were arrested. Gandhi spent four years organizing khadi centers in villages throughout India and was himself imprisoned several times for violating the Salt Law. After release from prison in 1933, he closed his two weeklies and opened *Harijan*, "The Children of God," whose pages he devoted to assisting the Untouchables. He travelled throughout out his homeland to raise money for their cause. For the remainder of his life, *Harijan* was the vehicle for his attempt to renew Hinduism, free India from British imperialism, and unite with Islam to preserve the Indian nation. By 1934, when he founded the All-India Village Industries Association, over five thousand villages had khadi centers.

The Gandhi-Irwin pact he brokered with the British viceroy in 1937 helped the poor immensely, and over 100,000 nonviolent protesters were released from jail. Later that year, Gandhi represented the Indian Congress in a London summit about democratic reforms in India. He was arrested by the new viceroy upon his return. Nine months later, he began a fast to the death if the members of Hinduism's lowest cast—the Untouchables—were denied the right to vote in the upcoming election. When elections finally took place in 1937, village voting provided Congress a sweeping victory. Gandhi commented, "India is still a prison, but the inmates elect their jailers."

While the British could do very little to prevent Gandhi from attaining his first two objectives, they did thwart his third goal. After World War II broke out in September 1939, the British viceroy ignored the offer of the Indian Congress to assist the war effort. By refusing to do anything during wartime that would aid India's advance to independence, Great Britain at first ignored and then suppressed all efforts by Indians to practice self-government. In 1942, Gandhi began a campaign to "Quit India," which demanded immediate independence. He was arrested along with his wife, who had become a more-than-able organizer, and his personal secretary and a leading co-worker, Mahadev Desai. Both Desai and Kasturbai died in detention; Gandhi was released in 1944. Winston Churchill, prime minister of Great Britain during the war, arranged a two-state solution to guarantee chaos in the sub-continent. His successor, Clement Attlee, officially announced the plan for partition in June 1947. Gandhi was assassinated soon after on January 30, 1948.

Rudolf Steiner gave indications of the past lives of various world historic figures in his lectures on *Karmic Relationships*. His indication of the past life of Hamlet has been explored in some detail. The idea that past lives do indeed help explain world historic events stands behind my book about the Founding Fathers of the United States, *A Sanctuary for the Rights of Mankind*, and such a book could also be written about the leaders at the time of the Civil War. Steiner also provided an indication about a past life of Gandhi. In a 1923 lecture to the teachers of the first Waldorf School, he held up the figure of Mahatma Gandhi as the ideal to which teachers should aspire. Steiner pointed to Gandhi's speech before the court in 1922 as exemplary of the spirit of truthfulness that teachers should seek to attain.

Gandhi himself did not appreciate the honorific, Mahatma, being applied to himself. He called it a curse. Many other people, including some important leaders, also opposed its use. They recommended that he be addressed by his first name, Mohandes. Some biographers tried to assemble the arguments against the use of Mahatma, as many and as weighty as they are. The basic idea against its use was discussed previously. The honorific "mahatma" generally refers to an ascended master, like Gautama Buddha. Gandhi's autobiography revealed nothing similar to being overshadowed by a divine being while sitting under a fig tree at the age of thirty.

The fact that Rudolf Steiner addressed Gandhi as a mahatma is also problematic. Steiner had criticized the Theosophical Society for foisting a requirement on its members to affirm the Star of the East and its absurd belief that the child Krishnamurti was the reincarnated Christ. Steiner withdrew from the Theosophical Society in 1912 owing to his opposition and formed the Anthroposophical Society. He also spoke out against false mahatmas that Annie Besant and others claimed upheld the view of Krishamurti's divinity. The proper way to understand Steiner's use of the honorific must emerge from what was said earlier about the Western masters—that they do not overshadow another human being when that person reaches the age of thirty, but that they are born, grow up, and lead a full life as a human being.

In his book *The Battle for the Soul*, Bernard Lievegoed explores the past lives and present missions of three of the "Western" masters. Sergei Prokofieff also discussed their past lives and present missions.[12] Prokofieff included three other Western masters, though they clearly could not have incarnated as Gandhi. Lievegoed described Parzival as one of those masters, and characterizes his future task as "breathing enthusiasm into large groups of people for social ideals…he or she will travel in the world and a bring about a change of attitudes in relation to social questions."[13] The appearance of nonviolent civil disobedience as a social movement actually began with Gandhi. Chart I illustrates Gandhi's possible past lives, building on Lievegoed's discussion of Parzival's earlier incarnations.

Certain events in Gandhi's life and some moral qualities in his character can be compared to events in Parzival's life qualities of character. Mohandes Gandhi was born in 1869. Parzival became Lord of the Grail in 869, a millennium earlier. When Parzival attempted to join the Knights of the

---

12 Sergei D. Prokofieff, *Rudolf Steiner and the Masters of Esoteric Christianity*. Wynstones Press: Stourbridge, England, 2018.

13 Bernard Lievegoed, *The Battle for the Soul*. Hawthorne Press: Stroud, UK, 1993. pp. 94-95.

CHART I

Possible Past Lives of Mahatma Gandhi

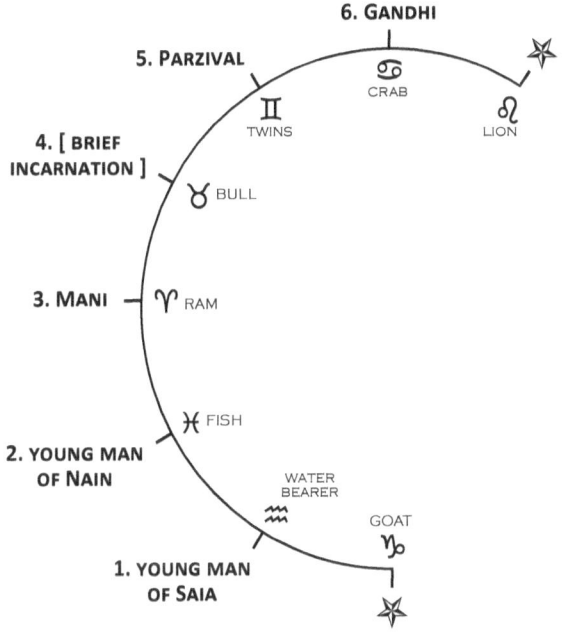

1. **YOUNG MAN OF SAIA** — logicism in pneumatism
2. **YOUNG MAN OF NAIN** — gnosticism in psychism
3. **MANI** — occultism in idealism
4. **BRIEF INCARNATION** — transcendentalism in rationalism
5. **PARZIVAL** — mysticism in mathematicism
6. **GANDHI** — empiricism in materialism

Round Table, he was driven away. He entered the Grail Castle and after many trials finally became a Grail knight. His task then became to show the Arthurian knights that the Grail cannot be won by striving for it, but only by grace. The knights of Arthur had to renounce being knights of the sword and become knights of the Word. In the ninth century, nonviolence could be attained by individuals. A thousand years later, it could become active in social movements, and leaders like Gandhi could bring the ideal of nonviolence to the nations of the world so that countries like India could begin to practice it.

Gandhi followed the religion of this parents, Hinduism, and entered into an arranged marriage at the age of thirteen. He became a tyrant to his child bride, and Kasturbai was kept in ignorance. Fortunately, another aspect of this Hindu custom allowed her to return to live with her parents six months each year. Gandhi did receive a formal education, and at age eighteen he journeyed to England to study law. These events are a reversal of those that Parzival went through. Parzival's mother, Herzeleid, raised him in a forest that shielded him from any contact with civilization. Parzival became a fool, ignorant of all social customs and responsibilities, a mirror, as it were, of what he imposed on Kasturbai.

When Gandhi went to London, he met the leaders of the Theosophical Society, Madame Blavatsky and Annie Besant, the most famous spiritual leaders in England. Both had strong ties with Eastern religions and with Hinduism in particular. When Parzival left Herzeleide, he sought out the fame of the knights of the Round Table and hoped to join them. Whereas

Parzival's foolishness made him a thing of sport for Arthur's knights, Gandhi realized that Besant wanted to use him to foster her Hindu credentials. Rather than joining the Theosophical Society, Gandhi was influenced to deepen his own understanding of Hinduism by reading the *Bhagavad Gita*.

Gandhi felt that the honorary title that he had been given, Mahatma, was actually a curse. The common view of Mahatma ("great atma," or the perfected spirit of man) in the Eastern world related it to the ascended masters, the six bodhisattvas or Eastern masters who had attained to Buddhahood. The last one to do so was Gautama Buddha, the founder of Buddhism in the sixth century B.C. Both biographers and many famous people who criticized Gandhi for not renouncing its use argued that Gandhi lacked the moral perfection that the honorific implied. Steiner's view of Parzival as a Master of Wisdom and the Harmony of Feelings can help explain this seeming contradiction. Western masters do not avoid all the tomfoolery associated with childhood and adolescence. Like Parzival, they have to take a human path through foolishness and doubt before attaining blessedness. The path of freedom requires the discovery of an inner guide since authority figures can no longer be blindly obeyed. The curse that Gandhi had to endure was to be seen as a mahatma—a leader whose authority was beyond question. His autobiography documented his many human failings, but his services to the spirit of Truth could not stop the all-too-human tendency of people to idolize their heroes. Like Gandhi, Parzival also suffered from a curse. When he returned to King Arthur's court in triumph to join their ranks, Cundrei challenged Parzival's right to do so. She told of his failure in the Grail Castle and cursed him for not helping Anfortas. Like Gandhi's curse, Parzival's was a reminder of his true mission.

Gandhi was remarkably honest. His autobiography demonstrated this moral quality in manifold ways. Its title plainly states that the arc of his life was basically a series of experiments with truth. When he bade the reader farewell after one-hundred-and-sixty-seven chapters, he explained that his study of religion and life had led him to the conclusion that God is Truth. When Steiner discussed Parzival's previous incarnation as Mani, he explained that as a human mahatma (i.e. as a Western master, not an Eastern one) he could experience himself as being over-lightened by the Spirit of Truth. Jesus Christ explained to His disciples that He had to go through crucifixion and death if he were to be able to send to them the Spirit of Truth, whom he also called the Advocate or Paraclete. Mani, as he went through this experience of the baptism by fire and the Holy Spirit, even called himself the Spirit of Truth.

Gandhi was also extremely shy. He was fine when speaking to friends and individuals, but when addressing a group, even writing out a speech did not help. Someone else would have to read it for him. Needless to say, his shyness caused him great difficulties as a lawyer. Research was not a problem, but pleading a case was impossible. Not until 1922, at the age of fifty-three, did Gandhi finally overcome his embarrassment and deliver what would become a world-historic speech, telling the presiding judge of his commitment to truth. A possible explanation for Gandhi's shyness can be found in the life of Parzival. Raised by his mother in the midst of natural surroundings and far away from all the trappings of civilization, Parzival was illiterate and ignorant of all customs and mores. When he left to become knight, he depended on sheer good luck and the kindness of strangers for his survival. Gurnemanz took him into his castle and trained him in the art of knightly combat and the code of chivalry. As Parzival awoke from his childish dream life, a deep-seated embarrassment at his rude and crude conduct took root in his soul. This shame sealed his lips at the same time as his behavior and bearing became more noble.

Gandhi's desire to serve the community, the poor, and the oppressed grew ever stronger throughout his life. In 1894 at his farewell dinner celebrating his legal victory for Abdulla, he could only think of the injustice being done to the Indians in Natal. Instead of returning to India, Gandhi stayed to fight for their rights and serve their many needs. He brought his family to South Africa in 1896 and home-schooled his children to insure that they would be instilled with this idea. When Tolstoy Farm began in 1912, he served as headmaster with the same ideal in mind. This particular moral quality characterized the family that traced its lineage back to Titurel. Parzival was a member of the Grail family and ascended to lead its task of serving all mankind by becoming Lord of the Grail.

Gandhi's path of self-development took him through the soul trials and led him to a deep study of certain modern works of literature. In 1893 he read Leo Tolstoy's *The Kingdom of God is Within You* and was overwhelmed. The secret of the Baptism by fire was revealed to him as the source of the independent thinking he sought to attain. Gandhi even reached out to Tolstoy and began a correspondence that lasted until Tolstoy's death in 1910. In 1912, he named his new project Tolstoy Farm in honor of the great Russian writer.

In 1903 Gandhi read a second modern work of literature that moved him as deeply as Tolstoy's had. John Ruskin's book *Unto This Last* was built on the same foundation of independent thinking and profound morality as Tolstoy's but extended into the social world. Gandhi studied Ruskin's essay and later translated it into Hindi with the title *Sarvodaya*, "The Welfare of All," which endeavored to transform Tolstoy's ideal of "passive resistance to evil" into an active transformation of society in order to help the poor and the oppressed. Gandhi finally decided to coin a new term for the activity of the Spirit of Truth in the social realm—"Satyagraha." What had begun as the Spirit of Truth's activity in the element of thinking could now enter the social realm and begin to give shape to the Blessed Community. When the time came to bring the blessings of the Holy Spirit back to India, Gandhi lived with his close friends and family in the Satyagraha Ashram so that the activity of the Spirit of Truth would be clearly visible for all to see.

The third step on this path of self-development also involved a book, but not one written in modern times. The *Bhagavad Gita* is certainly worth reading and is an object of study in many universities and seminaries. Gandhi, however, used it as an object of meditation. He began each day by memorizing lines from the *Gita*. He would then review the lines he had already memorized. Gradually he realized that passages from the thirteen chapters that he had memorized enabled him to understand the people he interacted with and to grasp the deeper meaning of the events of his daily life. The *Gita* became, as it were, his dictionary of life. A truly sacred book makes the daily life holy. Such a book is a creation of the Spirit of Truth, a fountain of knowledge for the people and the times for whom it is intended. Gandhi realized that as handicapped as he was by his deep-set shyness, he did have recourses to another mode of expression. By putting his thoughts down on a sheet of paper, Gandhi, with the aid of the Phoenix Settlement, began publishing *Indian Opinion*. Gandhi's articles in this weekly publication educated his readers about social issues and inspired them to take up the struggle against injustice. They were the soil in which Satyagraha could take root. In 1919, after returning to India, Gandhi entered the stage of self-development called Inspiration at the very time two weekly publications were offered to him for his use. Both *Young India* and *Navajivan* offered their readers the living thoughts of an active mind and the insights of a master.

In 1912, during the fourth stage of Gandhi's spiritual development, he founded Tolstoy Farm. This experiment in communal living enabled him to take on the role of headmaster. He put into practice his pedagogical ideas of eliminating corporal punishment and helping both the well-behaved and the unruly students to learn and work together. He concluded (in agreement with Steiner's pedagogy) that misbehavior and low achievement were a reflection of the teacher's failings, not the student. He went so far as to put himself on fasts to try to correct the situation. He also included the students in religious fasts to help develop an appreciation for the different faiths of members of Tolstoy Farm. Hindus, Parsis, and Muslims would all fast during Ramadan for example. Gandhi's belief in the unity of all religions may reflect his earlier incarnation as Mani, the founder of Manicheism, which joined its followers—Christian, Zoroastrian, and Buddhist—in a faith based on the ideals of peace and brotherhood. In his personal life, Gandhi took up the study of the Bible and the Koran to further his effort to embody the Spirit of Truth in his role as teacher.

When Gandhi and his family returned to India in 1915, he met the Indian political leader he most admired, Gokhale, and agreed to abstain from introducing Satyagraha into India by taking a vow of silence regarding it until he had familiarized himself with India's political situation. Not bringing Satyagraha into action did not mean that it had to be hidden, for he named the ashram that his closest followers and their families lived in the Satyagraha Ashram. When an "Untouchable" family asked if they could join, Gandhi, acting in the spirit of Satyagraha, asked the families if they approved and then brought the members of Hinduism's lowest cast into a state of equality with other castes and members of different faiths. For Gandhi, the deeper meaning of the unity of the world's religions included the necessary reforms that they must undertake in order to enter the modern age. For Hinduism, the reform of the caste system was a necessity. Just as Christianity had to reject slavery, so did Hinduism have to learn to view the members of the Untouchable caste as free human beings.

In 1918, when Mahatma Gandhi entered the fifth stage of his self-development, he had fulfilled Gokhale's restriction on talking Satyagraha and was preparing to bring about its awakening force to the people of India. Gandhi, however, wanted to retain the power that the vow of silence had brought to him. Following the eight-fold path of Buddhism, he decided that observing the vow of silence could be moved to Mondays, the day devoted to Right Word—speaking thoughtfully and avoiding gossip. By spending all of Monday in silence, Gandhi could gain amazing insights by focusing his powers of concentration on how his plans would unfold and influence various groups of people. For example, the peasants of India would be greatly helped by the Spinning Association, since they could make their own clothes and not have to buy them. The workers in England's textile mills, however, might have to undergo hardship. Gandhi contacted the union leaders, explained the situation of the Indian villagers, and received union support for his actions.

Gandhi also discovered that taking social action by practicing Satyagraha can lead to unintended grave errors, even to "Himalayan miscalculations." Seeing into the depths of the world requires an equally deep introspection into oneself. When his followers were provoked to violence, he did not blame them but rather blamed himself for not training them properly. Through the power of inspiration, Gandhi gathered supporters around him who could become the cadre of exemplars for others to follow. Just as religions need to enter the modern age and acknowledge the freedom of all people, so do the Satyagrahi have to bring their followers to freely embrace the sacred law within. This power of inspiration can also assist writers and help bring their readers into the modern age. The meditative exercise of silence on Monday made the written expression of Gandhi's analysis, research, and insights that much more inspiring.

The arc of Gandhi's activity in India resulted in his arrest and trial in 1922. His speech to the judge was presented by Steiner the following year as an exemplum of what a teacher should hope to achieve—becoming a vessel for the Spirit of Truth so that it may manifest in the world of mankind. The ideal teacher, imbued with the Spirit of Truth, enables the Holy Spirit to become active in the daily life. In 1925, Gandhi began the sixth stage of his self-development—the stage of intuition—by taking up the task of writing his autobiography. *The Story of My Experiments with Truth* showed how the Spirit of Truth ennobled the daily life and revealed it to be a sacred journey. The discovery of truth in the daily life is akin to what Gandhi's teacher Raychandbhai called self-realization: "to see God in every one of my daily acts." What Gandhi's spirit guide had earlier held up to him as the goal of his life's journey came back to him at this stage as spiritual communion with his fellow human beings and the revelations of the Spirit of Truth in the Blessed Community.

Rudolf Steiner's view of the Western Masters of Wisdom and the Harmony of Feelings emphasizes that they do not overshadow or incorporate themselves in other human beings, but rather lead a full life—complete with all its seeming disadvantages. In the present age of the consciousness soul, the unfolding of human freedom necessitated the withdrawal of the Father Spirit. In terms used by spiritual researchers, the human soul is the widow since the father is absent. The child born into this situation is called the son of the widow. Mani and Parzival were sons of the widow. Their actual familial connections reflected their spiritual state and their need to take up the path from ignorance to doubt, and finally to blessedness. Gandhi had to reject Raychandbhai as a guru. No authority could substitute for the Father Spirit that must be sought by kindling the light of active thinking.

The modern path of initiation requires a pioneer, a person to set foot on the earth freely and to accept the price of loneliness that comes with an active life of thought and a social conscience. Religious groups must assist the awakening of the God within, and not oppose the modern counterpart of experiencing the light of the Grail. Only from this source can the Blessed Community be formed. Even if the Albigenses, Waldenes, Cathars, and Knight Templars of medieval Europe were but temporary manifestations of the Blessed Community that will appear in the future and will be called the city of brotherly love, they were also stepping-stones that led to the Satyagraha Ashram.

Several important books have been written about the reincarnations of the historical figures in *Parzival*. Kirchner-Bockholt's book was discussed earlier, focusing on Schionatulander and Sigune. The former was the defender of Parzival's lands, the latter the childhood friend of Condwiramurs, Parzival's future wife. Sigune became Parzival's spirit guide, serving a role much like that of the hermit, Trevrizent. Together they reincarnated as contemporaries of Gandhi and took on leadership positions in the Anthroposophical Society. When Rudolf Steiner became president of the Society, Ita Wegman became a member of the governing council, the Vorstand. When Steiner discussed Schionatulander and Sigune in *Karmic Relationships*, he emphasized that they had needed to gain certain talents and abilities that could only be achieved by immersing themselves in the mystery stream of the Grail. By doing so, they had aided Parzival greatly in his quest to become Lord of the Grail. In 869, Parzival had founded the first path to the Grail Castle, and its secrets were offered to all mankind through Wolfram von Eschenbach's masterpiece, *Parzival*.

Steiner's other incarnations were also indicated in *Rudolf Steiner's Missions and Ita Wegman* (see chart B). In his Greek incarnation as Aristotle, Steiner brought philosophy into the world. His co-workers included Alexander, who helped spread Aristotalianism throughout the known worlds; Plato, who was Aristotle's teacher and anticipated the coming of philosophy with his *Dialogues*; and Socrates, who as Plato's teacher had issued the call to take up philosophy in 399 B.C. This group of four philosophers formed the tone of theism in ancient Greece.

Its importance was such that Steiner's last lecture was devoted to Karl Julius Schröer and his earlier incarnation as Plato. Steiner's research on Leo Tolstoy led him to suggest that Tolstoy was a later incarnation of Socrates. In his 1904 lecture on Manicheism, Steiner used Tolstoy's term—"passive resistance to evil"—to characterize the ideal of nonviolence that was at heart of the mystery stream of the Grail in modern times. The correspondence between Tolstoy and Gandhi about the idea of Satyagraha takes on a new dimension in light of the possibility of Gandhi being a reincarnation of Parzival. Just as Schionatulander assisted Parzival in laying the foundation stone of the Grail, so can Gandhi be accounted a co-worker of Steiner in laying the foundation stone of love. Genuine nonviolent social movements arose in South Africa and India as complements of the cultural unfolding in Europe of the spirit of Anthroposophia (the transformed spirit of Philosophia).

Walter Johannes Stein was another of Steiner's close companions. A biography by Johannes Tautz, *W.J. Stein*, helps to clarify the karmic relationship of Stein and Trevrizent. Stein's own research on *Parzival* was prompted by Steiner, who chose him to teach *Parzival* to the eleventh graders in the first Waldorf School. Stein published it in 1928 as *The Ninth Century and the Holy Grail*. His insights into the character of Trevrizent uncovered the reason for the former knight to become a hermit. By trying to overcome the sin of his brother Anfortas, he hoped to bring balance into the world and helped guide Parzival on his path to the Grail Castle. By understanding the needs of others, Trevrizent was able to find his own mission. When Stein was actually able to meet Gandhi, he brought with him as a gift Rudolf Steiner's *The Threefold Social Order*. As he had done in an earlier incarnation, he brought the best guidance he could find to the man who had worked so valiantly to inspire a social movement serving the needs of the poor and the oppressed. The economic transformation that needes to accompany social revolution is the theme of Steiner's book. Stein's abiding concern for others enabled him to bestow Gandhi with Steiner's insight into the threefold society, with its practical solution to the seeming contradiction between capitalism and socialism.

The Spear of Destiny by Trevor Ravenscroft is a third book presenting research on the reincarnations of the individuals in *Parzival*. Unfortunately, it is flawed. Ravenscroft was a student of Walter Johannas Stein for a brief period before Stein's death in 1957. Since I had read *The Spear of Destiny* in 1975 and became a member of the Anthroposophical Society in 1979, I was happy to meet two leaders of the Anthroposophy Society in America who were also students of Stein and who had known Ravenscroft personally. When I asked Werner Glas and René Querido about Ravenscroft's book, they both told me that it was a hodgepodge of Stein's insights with Ravenscroft's inaccuracies, written for the sake of sensationalism and to make money. Steiner's actual views about misguided Western secret societies and their plans involving the transition from the British empire to American commercialism and electronics (usually called Americanism) can be found in a long lecture cycle entitled *The Karma of Untruthfulness*. What makes *The*

Spear of Destiny so compelling is its focus on Adolf Hitler and the figure of Klingsor, the black magician who attacked the Grail knights and whose castle, Castle Marveil, was the evil counterpart of the Grail Castle.

Rudolf Steiner and the House of Anthroposophists took on a great task in the twentieth century. They sought to provide a path for all thinking human beings that would bring the Grail Castle within their purview through the Foundation Stone of Love. Walter Johannes Stein and the house of the Grail stream joined with Steiner to help him accomplish this daunting goal. Mahatma Gandhi took on the leadership of the social realm and started a movement in the tone of naturalism to offer hope that a truly human culture would emerge from the ashes of two World Wars (see chart J).

CHART J

The Grail Mystery Stream Aiding Rudolf Steiner

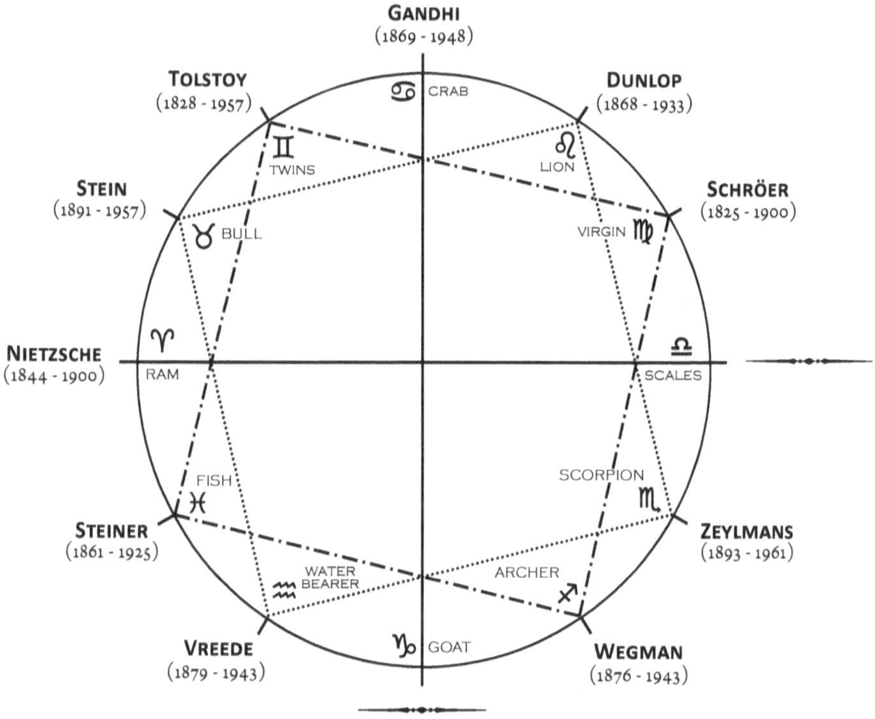

GANDHI (1869 - 1948) — CRAB

TOLSTOY (1828 - 1957) — TWINS

DUNLOP (1868 - 1933) — LION

STEIN (1891 - 1957) — BULL

SCHRÖER (1825 - 1900) — VIRGIN

NIETZSCHE (1844 - 1900) — RAM

SCALES

FISH

SCORPION

STEINER (1861 - 1925) — WATER BEARER

ZEYLMANS (1893 - 1961) — ARCHER

VREEDE (1879 - 1943) — GOAT

WEGMAN (1876 - 1943)

	tone of **theism** *thinking* ☉	tone of **intuitionism** *feeling* ☾	tone of **naturalism** *willing* ⊕
NORTH	LEO TOLSTOY	DANIEL DUNLOP	MAHATMA GANDHI
EAST	CARL JULIUS SHRÖER	WILLEM ZEYLMANS VON EMMICHOVEN	
SOUTH	ITA WEGMAN	ELIZABETH VREEDE	
WEST	RUDOLF STEINER	WALTER JOHANNES STEIN	FRIEDRICH NIETZSCHE

5.
Reverend Martin Luther King, Jr. and the Civil Rights Movement

Dr. King, in an intellectual autobiography entitled "Pilgrimage to Nonviolence," described his evolution from fundamentalism to liberalism while attending Crozer Theological Seminary from 1948 to 1951. In his senior year he took up the study of Reinhold Niebuhr and the American form of neo-orthodoxy. While he did not discard the social gospel of Rauschenbusch and its liberalism, the question of its viability had to be answered. The impasse between the liberalism of the social gospel and the neo-orthodox acknowledgment of the immoral behavior of companies and collectives of every sort, political and religious, led King to study modern philosophy and existentialism. He read Kierkegaard and Nietzsche, Jaspers and Heidegger, and concluded with Tillich's theology. Only when Dr. King explored Gandhi's life and teachings did an answer to the question of the viability of the social gospel begin to emerge. While Tillich may have stood on the boundary line between Liberalism and neo-orthodoxy, it was an intellectual stance. Gandhi lived there and showed Dr. King how a group of people can act for the good of all society.

Dr. King brought an intellectual appreciation of nonviolence to his new job in Montgomery, Alabama. Recently graduated and newly married, he became the minister of the

Dexter Avenue Baptist Church only two weeks prior to the landmark Supreme Court decision in Brown v. Board of Education on May 17, 1954. The Montgomery bus boycott began less than a year later. Out of necessity, Dr. King put his idea of nonviolence into practice. He experienced how the ideal of nonviolence led to a way of life filled with self-respect, courage, and strength for those who took it up. More importantly, he saw how it awoke the conscience in some of both those who had defended the Jim Crow laws and those who had gone along with them. It also provided a basis for reconciliation. Trials of the soul became redemptive, the spirit a living reality, and the Kingdom of God active in human thinking.

The pilgrimage to India that Coretta and Martin Luther King, Jr. embarked on in 1959 took them to the home of Mahatma Gandhi. They met the remaining members of the Satyagraha Ashram. Dr. King began to appreciate the independence of India, achieved without firing a single shot, as a world historic event. When the Civil Rights Movement began in earnest the following year, a further deepening occurred in King's understanding of nonviolent civil disobedience. By the summer of 1963, he could formulate the idea more fully. What Gandhi had called "Satyagraha," the power or force of the spirit of truth, Dr. King offered to the nation in his "Letter from Birmingham Jail."

Dr. King joined five other Civil Rights leaders in calling for a March on Washington to pressure Congress to pass the Civil Rights Act. He delivered a speech from the steps of the Lincoln Memorial that harkened back to the Great Emancipator's speech a century before. In "The Gettysburg Address" Lincoln had called for a new birth of freedom, which the defeat of slavery would bring. In the "I have a Dream" speech, Dr. King spoke of the manacles of segregation, the Jim Crow laws—and how the promise of freedom had yet to be fulfilled. He also recalled "The Declaration of Independence," Jefferson's masterpiece, which announced the entrance of Columbia onto the stage of world history on July 4, 1776. Its guarantee of the inalienable rights of life, liberty, and the pursuit of happiness to all men and women could not be withheld owing to skin color. King's speech took his predecessors' ideas one step further by offering a picture of what the realization of the proposition of the Founding Fathers, that all men are created equal, would look like. He envisioned an America where the dream of brotherhood took root and the Blessed Community began to arise, where religions joined together in harmony and the races in friendship and love.

Dr. King's birthday on January fifteenth has become a national holiday. His "I Have a Dream" speech is customarily read aloud to commemorate the Civil Rights Movement and its ideal. The speech shares this distinction with the Declaration of Independence, which is often read aloud on July fourth, and with the Gettysburg Address, which is read on Memorial Day. The Temple of Liberty, which the Founders envisioned, is upheld by three pillars evident on the National Mall—the Washington Monument, the Lincoln Memorial, and the Jefferson Memorial. The construction of the Martin Luther King, Jr. Memorial on the Mall shows the heights of renown that Dr.

King attained. Its location between the Jefferson and Lincoln Memorials reflects how his dream carried forward the twin visions that preceded his.

In 1964, King was awarded the Nobel Peace prize. His international stature rivaled that of Mahatma Gandhi. Although Gandhi did not win the Peace prize, the Nobel Academy affirmed that he deserved it by cancelling the 1948 award owing to his assassination. Winning the prize, however, did not exempt Dr. King from the assassin's bullet. His final speech, "I've Been to the Mountaintop," showed that he understood God's will and believed in the promise of the vision of the glory of the coming of the Lord.

Dr. King's intellectual development at Crozer Theological Seminary, and his study of Reinhold Niebuhr in particular, gave him the direct experience of leading a double life. King saw that the Social Gospel preachers were charlatans, while the Negro preachers tended to become spiritual profiteers. His study of Niebuhr lead also to an experience of having a spirit guide. Niebuhr's emphasis on a Gandhian approach to the evils of segregation encouraged King to take up studying Gandhi as well.

Dr. King tried to avoid the hypocrisy of the Social Gospel by leaving Atlanta and accepting an appointment as the minister in a church in Montgomery, Alabama. At age 26 he chose to support the court cause of Rosa Parks and lead a bus boycott in the city. Giving nightly speeches at the Dexter Avenue Church, he inspired the black community to sustain its boycott during the long months of negotiations and trial proceedings. King believed that following the path of nonviolence was due to an inner voice telling him to do what was right and giving him the courage to face anything. Even soul trials such as the bombing of his house became redemptive for himself, for his community, and for the policemen who marveled that King's belief could sway a frenzied crowd onto the path of peace.

Dr. King overcame the tradition of an otherworldly social gospel by founding the Montgomery Improvement Association. Negotiations to end segregation on buses were held with the municipal government. The NAACP offered to guide the Rosa Parks' case until it reached the Supreme Court. Their lawyers, along with many others, helped defend Dr. King and other leaders from the harassment and intimidation of white supremacist backlash. King's common-sense insistence on the use of nonviolent tactics won him support by awakening the conscience of many white people and providing the basis for reconciliation. Victory occurred after a year of litigation, in December 1956. The founding of the Southern Christian Leadership Conference (SCLC) that year further expanded the scope of nonviolent protest.

Dr. King met James Lawson at Oberlin College in 1957. Lawson had gone to India to learn about nonviolence from the remaining members of the Satyagraha Ashram but returned when he learned of Dr. King's bus boycott. A fellow black minister, though Methodist rather than Baptist, Lawson was not a mentor to King, like Reinhold Niebuhr or Paul Tillich, but a practitioner of nonviolence. During a serious conversation at

Oberlin, he convinced Dr. King to make a pilgrimage to India. In 1959, Dr. King studied nonviolence by personally meeting with the foremost followers of Gandhi. Like Reverend Lawson, he realized that Gandhism without Gandhi was but an empty shell. Gandhi's achievements, though, could then shine more brightly.

In the year following Dr. King's return to America, the nonviolent sit-in movement to get rid of Jim Crow laws began in earnest. Dr. King joined with James Lawson to speak to the students who would found the Student Nonviolent Coordinating Committee (SNCC), the only Civil Rights group with the word "nonviolent" in its name. Its members, black and white, attempted to form the Blessed Community. They strove for a leaderless group that would take action only after reaching consensus, that lived and worked together in the spirit of brotherhood.

In the early 1960's, Dr. King's mission to end segregation began to focus more directly on the issue of voter registration. The Southern Christian Leadership Association joined together with SNCC, the Congress of Racial Equality (CORE), and the NAACP to form the Council of Federated Organizations (COFO). Together they undertook the arduous and dangerous task of registering black voters in Mississippi. Demonstrations and protests often led to arrest for many, including Dr. King. While in Birmingham jail in April 1963, he wrote the letter that crystallized the mission of ending Jim Crow. He explained the four stages of nonviolent direct action and how it could be used to overthrow slavery's legacy. Liberal white people and middle-class black people needed to take the step of actively supporting the Civil Rights Movement. Dr. King's warning emphasized that this moral movement required an end to religious complacency.

Dr. King's speech in front of the Lincoln Memorial on August 28, 1963, compared the promise in the Declaration of Independence and the hope expressed in the Gettysburg Address with the reality of segregation. The written part of Dr. King's speech developed this comparison in detail. When he had finished and was ready to sit down, Mahalia Jackson said, "Martin, tell them about the dream." What King spoke about next came from his heart, and it changed the hearts of many who heard him. The idea that the Kingdom of God is within and that the Holy Spirit can become alive in a Blessed Community is the good news, the gospel that Dr. King was preaching. His mission to make a disciple of this nation, the United States of America, required him to form an imagination, a dream of peace and brotherhood, that would enable the Spirit of Truth to inspire all Americans. This task crowned the March on Washington and brought Dr. King's Memorial into alignment with the two memorials that it stands between.

The peacefulness of the March on Washington and the harmony of its participants, both black and white, made it an example of the virtue of tolerance that the speech extolled. Tolerance is the virtue of the water trial, and the Civil Rights Movement can be identified as America's water trial. The willingness to control feelings of dislike for a different racial group, to think positive thoughts towards its members and seek out the virtues of individuals, is the basis for the dream becoming a reality.

The SCLC had placed the burden of fund-raising on Dr. King's shoulders. The college lecture circuit and talks to unions and other progressive groups left him little time for the philosophical and religious studies that he had once pursued. With the sit-ins in 1960 and the marches and demonstrations that followed, King was arrested twelve times and his home was bombed twice. His pilgrimage to nonviolence quite rightly earned him international recognition, and he was awarded the Nobel Peace prize in 1964. The importance of the Selma march on "Bloody Sunday" in 1965, in which peaceful demonstrators were brutally beaten by police on the Edmund Pettus bridge, drew him back into the thick of nonviolent direct action. Dr. King took on the leadership role, and on March 9th he led the marchers on a second advance towards the five hundred Alabama state troopers blocking their way over the bridge from Selma to Montgomery. When their commander ordered the troops to withdraw, King had "but an instant to decide whether this was a trap or a miraculous parting of the Red Sea."[14] His decisiveness in turning around and leading the marchers back to the church resulted in him being roundly criticized. Yet violence was averted, and Dr. King led a successful march over the bridge two weeks later, which helped bring the nation together. Dr. King's speech on March 23rd,

---

14 Taylor Branch, *At Canaan's Edge*. Simon & Schuster Paperbacks: New York, 2007.

broadcast live to the whole country, reached deeply into the soul of America as the Spirit of Truth spoke through him.

The Civil Rights Act of 1964 and the Voting Rights Act of 1965 have been viewed as great victories marking the success of the Civil Rights Movement. As helpful as such laws may have been in ending Jim Crow in the South, they certainly did not affect the *de facto* segregation in Northern cities. Prizes and laws cannot substitute for the kind of organizing that Dr. King discussed in his letter from Birmingham jail, or that Gandhi practiced in India. Dr. King moved to Chicago in 1966 to attempt to open the housing market for black families living in the black belt of the most segregated city in America. The marches that he led clarified to him that Mayor Daley and the white residents of Marquette Park and Cicero were at least as difficult to win over as their counterparts in the South, if not more so.

Dr. King not only found opposition to granting black people their civil rights in Northern cities, but he also met opposition to his nonviolent methods among black people. In May of 1966, Stokely Carmichael took over the leadership of SNCC and expelled all of the white members. In the same year, Huey P. Newton founded the Black Panther Party. The Black Power Movement promoted a different method of organizing than the politically oriented direct-action programs of Dr. King and SCLC. It can be called community-based organizing.

Dr. King began building bridges to progressive movements throughout the country. He worked with organizers of poor people in towns and cities and on reservations, the majority of whom were white. His failures to make gains in Chicago did not deter him from challenging the federal government's policy of waging war in Southeast Asia. In 1967, he spoke out powerfully in opposition to the Vietnam War and formed a coalition, which he called the Poor People's Campaign, in an attempt to shift government spending away from the war machine's misadventure in Southeast Asia towards programs that would meet the needs of poor people. He laid out plans for a second March on Washington in the spring of 1968, determined that it would this time be one with staying power. The movement needed to advance to a higher level of organizing, one that inspired communities of poor people throughout the country to stand up for their rights. He envisioned a tent city like the one that Gandhi had helped construct in South Africa. His assassination on April 4th brought down the Poor People's Campaign. Just as Gandhism without Gandhi could not succeed in India, neither could the Poor People's Campaign without Dr. King.

The influence that Gandhi's ideals of *ahimsa* (nonviolence) and Satyagraha (truth) had on Dr. King suggests a karmic connection between them. The research on Parzival and his earlier incarnations (see chart I) can be supplemented by research by Walter Johannes Stein, published in 1928 as *The Ninth Century and the Holy Grail*. Stein developed the view that a full picture of the ideal of man in *Parzival* included two other characters in addition to Parzival. According to Stein, Sir Gawain, representative of the feeling life, and Feirefiz, representative of the will force, would need to join with Parzival, representative of the thinking life, to give a full picture of the ideal of humanity. Dr. King's dependence on Gandhi's ideas, in addition to the lead role he played in America's nonviolence social movement—complementary to that of Gandhi in India—could be viewed as a mirror of the aid that Parzival gave to Sir Gawain both before and during his trials at Castle Marveil. Dr. King's study of Niebuhr and of Gandhi, along with his pilgrimage to India, allowed him to take in the ideals of Gandhi freely, rather than like those of a guru (which Gandhi himself opposed). Dr. King's experience of the Blessed Community in Montgomery showed that he wasn't following an authority, but learning from life, which conformed to the ideal of existentialism.

Stein discussed the rumors of Gawain's wanton ways with women suggested in chapters seven and eight of *Parzival*. He explained that they were false in terms of Gawain's actual behavior. Spiritually, however, Stein suggests that these rumors did hold up the mirror to Gawain's impure thoughts. The FBI's illegal wire taps and leak of scandalous materials obtained through them were used by J. Edgar Hoover to tarnish Dr. King's public image. As unjustified as the federal government's actions were, they can perhaps be viewed as a necessary counterpoint to the rumors that Gawain himself also endured.

In 1957, James Lawson played a significant role in Dr. King's further steps towards developing a nonviolent movement in America. Lawson's efforts to deepen his own understanding of nonviolence and satyagraha led to creating courses and workshops that brought Gandhi's ideas to life for his students. In *Parzival*, Gawain's spiritual advance required him to win the wreath of virtue. Unfortunately, it also pitted him against another knight who had also done so. Parzival's task was to fight both of them individually to prevent their duel in order that they could become friends. Such strange karma may help explain the deep connection Lawson and King had to Gandhi and the powerful influence they had on one another.

Dr. King's March on Washington can perhaps become more understandable if it is related to Gawain's entrance into Castle Merveil which followed the trial of the wreath of virtue. Malcolm X's characterization of Dr. King's action as the Farce on Washington points to an unstated element that needs to be recognized. While Klingsor himself was not present in Castle Merveil, his influence there was palpable. The same was true of Washington, D.C. The passage of two major pieces of civil rights legislation showed that reform was possible, but the plans for the Southern strategy, the gentrification of Northern cities, and expansion of the military-industrial complex were not affected. Dr. King's last march, a mass march planned in Memphis in early April of 1968, has no memorable speech or Nobel peace prize associated with it—only an assassin's bullet before it could even start, and a coverup to follow. The murder of Dr. King on April 4th rings out like an echo of Gandhi's murder in 1948. (See chart K)

CHART K

A Possible Past Life of Dr. Martin Luther King, Jr.

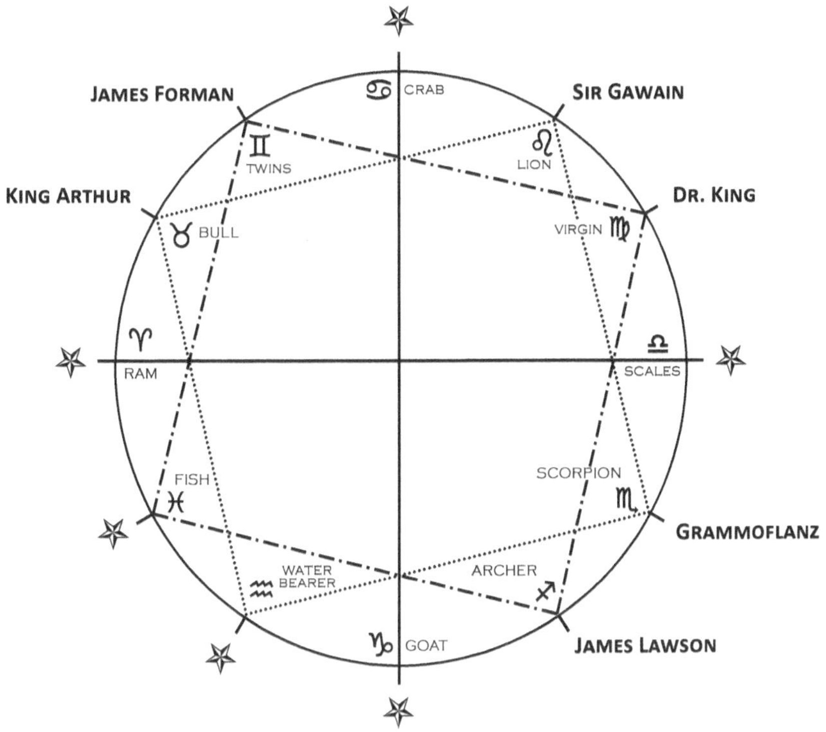

	tone of theism *sun* ☉	tone of intuitionism *moon* ☾
NORTH	JAMES FORMAN	SIR GAWAIN
EAST	DR. KING	GRAMMOFLANZ
SOUTH	JAMES LAWSON	✦
WEST	✦	KING ARTHUR

The comparison of the plot of Hamlet to the events in the American Civil War and to those in the Trojan War, outlined in chapter two, shows remarkable similarities in all three wars. A comparison of the same events in the Civil War to events in the Civil Rights Movement helps to clarify the great reversal that occurred a century later. The violence of war gave way to the nonviolence of civil disobedience. The Kansas-Nebraska Act of 1854, a legislative act, is credited with provoking the Slave Power conspiracy to send Southern settlers to Kansas to vote in the election there about whether the territories of Kansas and Nebraska would be slave or free when they became states. The terror that they unleashed led John Brown and his small band of armed men to retaliate. Brown's victories in Kansas were a stepping-stone to his next attempt to provoke an uprising against slavery by attacking a federal arsenal at Harper's Ferry. He planned to use the weapons seized to arm slaves and begin a guerrilla war. His capture and quick execution in December 1859 were a sacrifice he willingly made.

The corresponding event a century later began with a judicial decision. In "Brown v. The Board of Education," the Supreme Court ended the separate-but-equal doctrine, getting rid of the legal basis for the segregation of schools in America. This victory of NAACP lawyers inspired many people, but especially Rosa Parks, the field secretary of the NAACP office in Montgomery. Her arrest for refusing to move to the back of the bus less than a year later was the trial case that the NAACP was looking for in order to expand the Supreme Court's ruling on desegregation. Dr. King's leadership of the

Montgomery bus boycott was important, but his insistence on nonviolence, even when his house was fire-bombed with his family inside, showed how completely the ideal of *ahimsa* had taken root in his soul. In 1959, to show the depth of his commitment, Dr. King made his pilgrimage to India to honor the sacrifice of Gandhi and understand his path of Satyagraha better.

The second event of the Civil War involved the secession of the Southern states in 1860 and the formation of the Confederacy in 1861 with Jefferson Davis as president. Confederate secession can be compared to the abduction of Helen, the spirit of Greece, at the beginning of the Trojan War. It is ironic that Menelaus, the husband of Helen who suffered such indignity, became the leader of the rebels who sought to rend the union of states and abduct the spirit of America, Columbia. The protests against the Jim Crow laws in the South began in earnest a century later. The sit-ins at segregated lunch counters began in 1960 in Greensboro, North Carolina and soon spread throughout the same Southern states that had formed the Confederacy. The young people whose grandparents had once been slaves joined with liberal and progressive white people to oppose the unjust laws of segregation. Nonviolent civil disobedience became the means of recovering the rights that legally belong to all people. The Civil Rights Movement attempted to reverse the South's decision of a hundred years before and force southern states to live up to the U.S. Constitution.

In 1861, a week after Jefferson Davis claimed the leadership of the Slave Owner's States of America, Lincoln took the oath of office in Washington, the District of Columbia. By swearing allegiance to the Constitution of the United States, Lincoln took on the task of preserving the Union. Lincoln's oath mirrors the oath that Helen's suitors had sworn—that they would come to her aid and protect her. The mirroring of this even in the Civil Rights movement occurred among the youth organizers. The students in James Lawson's courses on nonviolence studied Mahatma Gandhi and the ways in which injustice could be overcome nonviolently. As the time approached to take these ideas out into the world and discover if they were practical, a more intensive study of certain fundamental tenets occurred. A kind of role-playing took place in Lawson's classes to ensure that the cadre and leaders of this movement would have sufficient training to act nonviolently and serve as an effective example that could help move the nation away from white supremacy. In April of 1960, Dr. King and Lawson met with student representatives who were preparing to form an organization dedicated to the ideals of nonviolence, brotherhood, and leadership by consensus. They formed the Student Nonviolent Coordinating Committee, with John Lewis serving as chairman, making a notable step towards bringing what Dr. King called "The Blessed Community" into reality.

The first major conflict of the Civil War occurred in July of 1861 at the Battle of Bull Run, when freshly trained Union troops marched in high spirits from the North to fight the Confederate army on an open field in Virginia. The Confederates won a victory that day near Manassas, signaling a long war ahead. A century later, Freedom Riders rode down from the North in an attempt to make the federal government enforce interstate transportation laws in the South. James Farmer, the chairman of the Congress of Racial Equality (CORE), organized the Freedom Rides. His army was composed of nonviolent conscientious objectors, who stirred the conscience of this land. Their victory was a reversal of General Stonewall Jackson's at Mannassas, since it was not in the support of slavery, but for freedom, as the name of the rides suggests.

The Confederate victory at the first Battle of Bull Run provoked much consternation in the ranks of Union generals. President Lincoln felt compelled to take up the study of military strategy himself (he had the Congressional library at his disposal), and in the winter of 1861 he did just that. He found a sound way to oppose General Lee's defensive strategy, but his generals disagreed with his unorthodox tactics. In a reflection of the argument between King Agamemnon and Achilles at the start of the *Iliad*, President Lincoln's ideas were thwarted by his generals. A century later, in 1961, James Forman developed a plan to push the federal government to enforce the U.S. Constitution and reverse the Hayes Compromise, which had ended Lincoln's vision of Reconstruction of the South by precipitously withdrawing federal troops. By building up tension and bringing into the open the contradiction between Jim Crow segregation laws and the written law of the land, Forman's plan forged a path forward for the Civil Rights Movement. Doing the reverse of arguing about strategy and tactics, the movement's leaders took direct action towards ending legal segregation.

In 1862, the Army of the Potomac fought a series of losing battles against the Army of Northern Virginia. General Robert E. Lee easily out-maneuvered the Union generals—some of whom, like Rosecrans, were incompetent, while others, like McClellan, were worse. General Lee, the reincarnated King of Troy, was ever victorious, as his son Hector had once been. A hundred years later, the civil rights groups—SCLC, SNCC, CORE, and the NAACP—sent their foremost organizers to Mississippi, where they formed the umbrella organization of the Council of Federated Organizations (COFO). Bob Moses coordinated the work of COFO on voter registration. In a reversal of the Civil War, COFO focused on the ballot, not the bullet.

The climax of the Civil War occurred on September 22, 1862, when Lincoln announced his intention to issue the Emancipation Proclamation. He had been waiting for a Union victory, which was finally achieved at Antietam. The Union general, McClellan, actually possessed General Lee's battle plans, making his victory easy to understand. The Emancipation Proclamation, issued on New Year's Day 1863, freed all slaves held in Confederate lands. It weakened the home front of the Confederacy and permitted black men to serve in the Union Army, which eventually swelled the ranks by over 200,000 soldiers. The Proclamation can be compared to the theft of the Palladium by Odysseus, which stole away the protection of Athena from the city of Troy and led to its destruction.

The corresponding event of the Civil Rights Movement occurred in April of 1963. Like Lincoln's proclamation, it was not a battle, march, or demonstration, but a letter. Dr. King's

"Letter from Birmingham Jail" revealed the four stages of the nonviolent struggle for justice in Birmingham, Alabama. It provided a blueprint for the Civil Rights activists, an explanation of how to organize and achieve meaningful victories on the path to justice. Dr. King also warned that the complacency of the religious establishment and of the middle class were the twin dangers to achieving the overthrow of slavery's legacy. His letter was a reversal of Odysseus's theft of the Palladium. Rather than use a talisman, like a wooden horse deployed to trick the Trojans, Reverend King spoke the truth—gathered in a decade of boycotts, sit-ins, and protests—and directed it to the heart of the Civil Rights activists whose free deeds would carry the movement forward.

The falling action of the Civil War commenced with General Lee's response to the Emancipation Proclamation. He invaded the North and attempted to capture Washington, D.C. General Meade led the Army of the Potomac and intercepted Lee at Gettysburg, Pennsylvania. The Battle of Gettysburg, fought over the course of three days before Independence Day in 1863, proved to be the counterpoint of Lee's victories the previous year. He received a crushing defeat. Ironically, Meade—who as the Greek king had sent his troops out to battle without their champion, Achilles, and who in his next incarnation as Fabius earned the name of "the Delayer" for repeatedly refusing to go into battle against the reborn Hector—won the Unioin's greatest victory by nothing more than defend the high ground at Cemetery Ridge. President Lincoln travelled to the battlefield in November and delivered "The Gettysburg Address" to commemorate the sacrifice of over 20,000 union soldiers to the cause of freedom. The war was not over, but the opportunity for the South to win on the battlefield was now closed to them, just as the opening for the Trojans to wage open battle had closed with the defeat of Hector.

One hundred years after Gettysburg, Dr. King and five other Civil Rights leaders organized the March on Washington, which took place on August 28, 1963. Not an army intending battle, but tolerant, nonviolent black and white Americans marched in unity, intent on rallying support for the Civil Rights Act. The speech Dr. King delivered that day embodied the hopes of those present for the ideal of brotherhood and for the Blessed Community that America was struggling to become. Just as Columbia spoke through Abraham Lincoln a hundred years earlier, so did the Spirit of Truth ring forth from the steps of the Lincoln Memorial as Dr. King intoned the words of "I Have a Dream."

In March of 1864 President Lincoln conferred the rank of lieutenant-general on Ulysses S. Grant—the rank that George Washington had also received. The strategy that Lincoln had worked on since 1861, which had grown into an idea that he called "total war," now had an eager recipient. The commander of all the Union armies could hardly wait to share Lincoln's strategy with the new general of the Western armies, William Tecumseh Sherman. General Grant had one talent that uniquely qualified him for this high office. As his *Personal Memoirs* clearly demonstrate, Grant personally knew both the officers in his army and those in the Confederacy. His knowledge provided him insights into their strengths and weaknesses. Fighting with such officers or against them enabled him to employ his own officer's strengths or—the reverse of the same coin—to use his opponents' weaknesses against them. Grant also knew that only he could oppose Lee on the field of battle and emerge the victor. The arguments that Lincoln had had with his other generals were no longer a problem since the new lieutenant-general, like Odysseus of old, had a both plan and the means of bringing it to fruition.

A similarly drastic change of direction occurred in the Civil Rights Movement a century later. By June of 1964, Malcolm X had changed his name to El-Hajj Malik El-Shabazz and had formed the Organization of Afro-American Unity (OAAU). His strategy involved internationalizing the Civil Rights struggle and emphasizing human rights. After withdrawing from the Nation of Islam, Malcom X had grown in stature. The possibility of collaboration between himself and Dr. King, like Lincoln and Grant's partnership a century before, inspired many activists and organizers to believe that a victory over white supremacy could be won.

After General Grant unified the lines of the Union army, he ordered a general advance and sent Major-general William Tecumseh Sherman into Georgia with orders to attack General J.E. Johnston. General Johnston had faced Grant at Vicksburg, a months-long siege that ended in a Confederate surrender the day after the Union victory at Gettysburg. He now opposed Sherman, making him one of the least fortunate of Confederate generals. Whereas the rising action of the Civil

War saw Union soldiers flee from defeat at the first Battle of Bull Run, the Battle of Atlanta in September brought a forced retreat of Confederate troops. General Johnston surrendered the Atlanta and all his military supplies and railroads rather than endure the loss of his entire army, as he had done during the siege of Vicksburg. When General Sherman finally left Atlanta to begin his March to the Sea, he had his men set fire to the Confederate supply dumps to prevent Johnston from re-arming his troops. Without waiting for the fires to burn out, Sherman left Atlanta. The fires did not die out as expected, but spread, and Atlanta burned—a strange and horrible repetition of the downfall of Troy.

The corresponding events in the Civil Rights Movement happened during the summer of 1964, known as Freedom Summer. It took place in Mississippi one hundred years after Sherman's invasion of Georgia and represented the culmination of Bob Moses's work with COFO, which had begun in 1961. Once again white students were encouraged to participate—not through a sit-in or march, but rather a voter registration drive. The racist opposition to this effort to bring black people into the arena of electoral politics was ferocious, but it could not prevent the formation of the Mississippi Freedom Democratic Party. When the leader of its delegation, Fanny Lou Hamer, spoke in front of the Credentials Committee of the Democratic Party, she clearly articulated why the walls of segregation had to come down. President Lyndon Johnson cut her off, then proceeded to strong-arm the MFDP by sending in spies and having the police harass its members.

President Johnson even eliminated the Mississippi delegation from the Democratic National Convention, ensuring that such Civil Rights activists would not have a public platform from which to express their views. With his other hand, President Johnson applied pressure on Congress to pass the Civil Rights Act. In July of 1964 he signed the act right before the opening of the Democratic National Convention. Not a military victory, but a political one helped to protect the civil rights of those people who were deemed second-class citizens by the Jim Crow laws of the South.

Two of the main events concluding the Civil War occurred within a week of each other in April of 1865. The assassination of Abraham Lincoln at the hands of John Wilkes Booth was a repetition of "The Mousetrap," the play that Hamlet used to catch the conscience of the king. The reincarnated Claudius used a gun to pay back the reincarnated Hamlet for the pain that he had caused him. Lincoln's death may also have reflected the murder of Agamemnon, which brought the Trojan War to its end. The assassination of El-Hajj Malik El-Shabazz (Malcolm X) in New York in February 1965 can be compared to that of Lincoln. Though Booth had a personal reason for his actions, historians also connect his nefarious deed to the plotting of certain secret societies, like the KKK, which appeared soon after the President's death to thwart Lincoln's vision for Reconstruction. Malcolm X had been a member of such a secret society, and felt the attack directed at him was more than just a vendetta by the Nation of Islam.

The second event that brought the Civil War to a conclusion was the end of hostilities, which occurred on the Sunday before with the surrender of General Lee to General Grant at Appomattox. It was the counterpoint of Jefferson Davis's secession and, for the South a least, a kind of repetition of the funeral of Ophelia—a grief filled burial of the sons of slave owners, the flower of the Confederacy. The counterpart of Lee's surrender occurred one hundred years later in Selma, Alabama, in March of 1965. The sit-ins of 1960, the Freedom Rides of 1961, and the marches and protests throughout the South culminated in Bloody Sunday—the clubbing of John Lewis and the police riot on the Edmund Pettus Bridge. When Dr. King arrived in Selma, he took charge, cancelled the second march, and then embarked on a third march two weeks later. This march wound slowly over the course of a week from the bridge in Selma to the governor's office in Birmingham. It was capped by Dr. King's speech, broadcast to the nation and filled with the forces of healing. The route taken by those thousands of marchers has since become a national historic trail.

The actual fulfillment of Lincoln's vow upon taking the oath of office played out over the entire course of the year in 1865. In January, Lincoln employed his considerable Presidential influence to get Congress to pass the thirteenth amendment to the Constitution through both the House and the Senate. By December, three-fourths of the states had voted in favor of the amendment, joining it to the Constitution as the law of the land. The ratification of the thirteenth amendment meant that slavery was outlawed throughout the country, and that Lincoln's promise in 1861 to uphold the Constitution now meant rejecting slavery. A similar bill came before Congress a century later—the Voting Rights Act. The devotion of the Civil Rights organizations to voter registration drives bore fruit. Now elected as President and no longer under constraint of a political campaign, Lyndon Baines Johnson used arm-twisting, pork-barreling, and other means to get it passed through both houses of Congress. He signed the Voting Rights Act into law in August of 1965.

One of Dr. King's most important followers, John Lewis, wrote an autobiography, *Walking With the Wind*, about his experiences in the Civil Rights Movement. He discussed the courses on nonviolence led by James Lawson that he had began taking in 1958 at the age of seventeen. He reviewed the founding of SNCC in 1960 and his activities as its executive secretary until the time of his resignation in 1966 at the age of twenty-six. The first stage of his development occurred in his teenage years and involved the study of Niebuhr, Thoreau, and Gandhi. The ideals of Satyagraha, love, and the Blessed Community that Reverend Lawson discussed in a living way made it clear to the students that their responsibility was not to approach these ideals intellectually, but to apply them in their everyday life.

When the sit-in movement began in Greensboro in 1960, Reverend Lawson explained to his students that they were responsible for leading the Nashville sit-ins that would soon take place. Under the banner of consensus, Lewis joined with Diana Nash, James Bevel, and other fellow students to form the Nashville Student Movement (NSM). He took on the task of summarizing the key ideas that all activists must understand and arranged workshops to help them prepare for the hatred and harassment they would soon face. In April of the same year, Lewis played a key role in the founding of a second Civil Rights organization, the Student Nonviolent Coordinating Committee. Like the NSM, it was dedicated to the ideal of overcoming the tradition of a group leader and his followers, and of having a cadre dedicated to practicing nonviolence. SNCC also brought black and white members together in harmony in an attempt to bring the Blessed Community into the earthly realm, in however temporary and partial a way.

Lewis found time the following year to join with James Farmer and CORE to participate in the first Freedom Rides. When the bus he was riding in stopped in Birmingham, he was beaten, arrested by Bull Connor's police, then taken to the Alabama border and left there. That same year, Lewis worked in Mississippi with COFO's voter registration campaign. The tradition of not allowing black people to register, let alone vote in the South, was so firmly entrenched that even by 1965 only 2% of the eligible black population was on the voter rolls. Ten years after the passage of the Voting Rights Act, that number had risen to 60%. In 1963, John Lewis, then the executive secretary of SNCC, was chosen to address the crowd gathered on the Washington Mall for the March on Washington. With the help of James Forman, Lewis was able to revise a speech that A. Philip Randolph had felt was too radical. He delivered "One Man, One Vote" to the enthusiastic assembly, a speech that on any other day would have been singled out for its importance. The speaker who followed him, however, was his idol, and the power of his oratory marked the event in history and memory. Lewis was more than content that the ideas he had expressed could become, perhaps, an important legacy of that momentous day.

Barely a week after the enactment of the Voting Rights Act in August 1965, the Watts riot erupted. John Lewis realized that organizing in the large cities outside of the South was wanting and that the movement itself would have to change in order for it to continue. He was not prepared, however, to accept the kind of change that leaders like James Forman and Stokely Carmichael were advocating. The difference between Freedom Now and Black Power was not a bridge he could cross. In May of 1966, Stokely Carmichael replaced him as executive director of SNCC. John Lewis turned to the Field Foundation and other not-for-profit organizations to earn a living. In 1982, he won an election to the Atlanta city council, and in 1986 to the United States House of Representatives, where he worked until his death in 2020.

6.
Nelson Mandela and the Anti-apartheid Movement in South Africa

In 1974 while in prison on Robben Island, Nelson Mandela decided to write his autobiography. At the age of fifty-six, he took on the same task that Gandhi had resolved to accomplish at the very same age. Gandhi's achievement was aided by the fact that he had a weekly newsletter, *Navajivan*, in which his articles could be published. Gandhi's autobiography was written over three years and had one hundred and sixty-seven installments. Steiner's autobiography was written in a similar way over a period of seventy weeks and published in *The Goetheanum News* in seventy installments. Mandela's *Long Walk to Freedom*, however, was written under the most trying conditions. He had to hide the manuscript from the warden, write secretly at night, review the comments and criticisms from Ahmed Kathrada and Walter Sisulu, have Mac Maray transfer Mandela's writing into microscopic shorthand which Maray then smuggled out of prison when he was released in 1976. After his own release in 1990, Mandela resumed work on his autobiography, bringing it up to date and publishing it in 1994.

Mandela was born on July 18, 1918, in Umtata, the capital of Transkei, to a chief of the Thebu tribe. He grew up in the Xhosa tradition. His father died when he was nine. In keeping with tribal tradition, Mandela underwent initiation and became a man at age sixteen. In 1933 he attended Clarkebury Methodist high school, and in 1937 he moved to Healdtown College. In 1939 he went to Fort Hare where he met Oliver Tambo. After joining the Student Representative Council, he became involved in a food boycott and was suspended from school.

When Nelson Mandela returned home, his regent, Jongintaba, ordered him to return to school as well as to submit to an arranged marriage. Mandela's rebelliousness opposed the racist customs of South African society and the Xhosa social traditions as well. With his older brother, Justice, he fled his homeland and entered the modern urban life of Johannesburg. In 1941 he worked for a law firm in Alexandra. He came under the positive influence of Walter Sisulu, even staying at times at his home. Walter Sisulu took on the role that Raychandbhai had served for Gandhi and that James Lawson would serve for Reverend King—that of spirit guide and trusted adviser. The following year Mandela began to attend meetings of the African National Congress with Walter Sisulu. In 1943 he met Anton Lembede at Sisulu's home and joined them on a visit to Dr. Xuma, the head of the African National Congress (ANC). They attempted to renew the ANC's tradition by organizing a Youth League. At age twenty-five Mandela became a member of the executive committee of the ANC's Youth League when it was founded on Easter of 1944.

In his autobiography, Mandela told of the double life that a black South African had to lead. The legal separation of the races in South Africa was comparable to the segregation that Dr. King would endure while living under the Jim Crow laws. Since Great Britain did not want criticism from the world community of nations for these policies, they made a serious attempt to create a black elite. Mandela saw their effort for what it was—giving a few token jobs to greedy, selfish intellectuals willing to sell out their race. He also realized that he could not find any real protection through such a job. Becoming a lawyer did not free him from harassment any more than working in a law office had. Trying to fight for justice and freedom actually brought down more repression.

Nelson Mandela's marriage to Evelyn Masa showed a decided lack of common sense. Instead of him feeling a need to find a job and provide for his family, his family became secondary to his political activities. Evelyn became the breadwinner. Instead of helping her with childcare and chores, Mandela devoted himself to the struggle. By 1950 his eldest son, Thembi, then five years old, asked Evelyn where Daddy lived. As they drifted apart, Evelyn upgraded her nursing certificate, bore another child, and became involved with the Jehovah's Witnesses. When Mandela was arrested and imprisoned for two weeks in 1956, he returned to an empty house. Evelyn had moved out and taken the children.

Mandela did make an attempt to earn a living by getting his law degree and opening a law office with Oliver Tambo in 1952. His legal colleague was also a fellow member of the ANC, and their collaboration provided leadership for the organization until Tambo's death in 1993. Their law office was the only black law office in South Africa, and it was respected and admired by the black people of Johannesburg for its competence and compassion. It was equally hated and reviled by the court system and harassed so greatly by the authorities that Mandela and Tambo had to close their office. Mandela's legal studies, however, were helpful in grasping the background for the apartheid laws of the 1950's. He was able to gain the insight as early as 1954 of where the courts and the political system as a whole were headed. Just as Gandhi's studies of Tolstoy and Ruskin bore fruit with his idea of satyagraha, so did Mandela's studies lead him to see the coming of a police state.

Mandela took up his mission of renewing the African National Congress in 1946. He worked with J.B. Marks, the president of the African Mine Workers Union, on a strike that was brutally repressed. In the process he gained tolerance for the communist union leaders just as he did shortly thereafter for the nonviolent protests of NIC and the Indian people against the Asiatic Tenure Act. The following year he was elected to the executive committee of the Transvaal ANC which he saw as a milestone of his commitment to the organization. By 1950 he was co-opted into the executive committee of the ANC. He was then chosen to help implement the Doctors' Pact which laid a foundation for cooperation between ANC and NIC. Working with Manilal Gandhi helped Mandela gain a deeper respect for both the eldest son of Gandhi and Gandhism itself. He discovered that Mahatma Gandhi himself believed that nonviolence was a tactic to be used as the situation demanded, and not when it was self-defeating. The

Defiance campaign protested against the apartheid laws. It brought black people and Indian people together, the very outcome that the apartheid laws were designed to prevent. In 1952 when Luthuli became president of the ANC, the goal of the Youth League was realized—to renew the ideals of the ANC in the hearts and minds of African youth and to find a dynamic leader to inspire them.

Mandela began viewing the problems of South African society as more than legal or political issues, but as cultural challenges as well. A 1953 law made the racist educational system much worse than before. He also viewed religion as hypocritical for refusing to respond to such immoral actions, and even supporting them. He criticized grassroots and even community organizations like the ANC for not meeting people on their own terms. In 1954 the ANC protested the government's decision to remove 80,000 from the slums of Johannesburg. ANC speakers spoke to crowds of people in Freedom Square, a part of the slum that was designated for demolition. They told their supporters that their voice would be heard, but never laid plans for a new location which would become necessary on February 9, 1955. The people's hopes were dashed, and the movement was shown to be impractical.

The organizing efforts of the ANC included forming the Congress of the People, which brought many different racial and political groups together to write the Freedom Charter. Mandela had been banned from attending political meetings. He continued speaking but in secret. The government finally decided to rid itself of the ANC altogether. In December 1956 one hundred and forty-four people were arrested and tried for treason. All of the leaders of the ANC were defendants. The trial was a farce, and the judge could do nothing but find the defendants to be innocent based on the flimsy evidence and self-contradictory testimony. The trial did, however, confirm Mandela's insight that a police state was coming. In 1960 at Sharpeville, the police massacred 69 protesters and left over 400 people wounded. The ideal of nonviolence is ineffectual when used against a racist army of police with orders to kill. The ANC proceeded with a large-scale protest against this massacre anyway. The ANC leadership was out on bail and waiting for a resumption of the treason trial at this time. They decided to send Oliver Tambo out of South Africa. Regardless of the trial's outcome, the ANC could remain active, even if it were in a foreign country. The not-guilty verdict came on March 29, 1961, over four years after Mandela's arrest. It showed how pathetic the state's case actually was, and it convinced the government to never let it happen again.

The verdict of not guilty convinced the executive committee of the ANC to go underground. Going underground meant turning into a creature of the night and becoming invisible. Nelson Mandela called his experience from April 1961 to August 1962 being the Black Pimpernel. Mandela and the High Command had started the Spear of the Nation (MK, or Umkhonto we Sizwe) despite having no experience in guerrilla warfare and not knowing how to live underground. They made many mistakes. Mandela's basic error was that he tended to stay in one place too long. Their first major action was a "stay-at-home" protest on May 29th. It seemed to make sense that a work stoppage would not endanger the lives of protesters. The state, however, reacted hysterically and raided all of the ANC offices. The state called up all of its police force and its army as well. One event, however, did inspire the ANC supporters: the selection of Chief Luthuli, the president of the ANC, to be the recipient of the Nobel Peace prize. He was to return to South Africa on December 16, Gingane's Day, the day the Boers defeated Gingane, the half-brother of Shaka, and leader of the Zulus. The High Command thought it was appropriate to celebrate Chief Luthuli's victory with three acts of sabotage that took no innocent lives. Early in 1962, Mandela escaped from South Africa and travelled throughout Africa, receiving training in the use of military equipment and in guerrilla tactics. He even met Oliver Tambo. Soon after his return to South Africa, he was captured.

Mandela blamed himself for the arrest, which included the capture of Walter Sisulu. He was charged with incitement to strike and a lack of travel documents. He emulated Mahatma Gandhi by speaking truthfully to the judge, who gave Mandela a five-year sentence. Less than a year later the 90-day detention law went into effect. This law allowed the police to arrest anyone they thought needed to be behind bars without formally charging them and to keep them in jail for three months. After 90 days the policeman could remand the prisoner for another 90 days, and so on, indefinitely. The police state was now complete, and it featured the regular torture of prisoners who were never charged or released.

The High Command of the Spear of the Nation (MK) was arrested in July 1963. Mandela was added to the group of people who were charged with sabotage. The state wanted to avoid the mistakes of the treason trial. The experts whom they called to testify would actually be competent, and the agent provocateurs whom they had planted would provide real evidence. The Rivonia Trial, as it came to be called, began in October. The prosecution case was then presented with the expectation that its success would result in the death penalty being imposed. The defense case began in April 1964 and rested on the idea that a truthful admission of the reason for sabotage and guerrilla war would be best. The world press was eagerly following the trial and speaking to that audience would be better for the defendants than telling lies and renouncing their actions that would probably not alter the preordained sentence anyway. Even so, the defense team and many defendants were shocked by Mandela's speech and counseled him to tone it down. He included some of it in his autobiography, and its similarity to Gandhi's speech at his trial in 1922 is remarkable. When the judge found them guilty and sentenced them to life imprisonment, the defendants concluded they had escaped death due to the influence of the world press.

The dark years on Robben Island involved government suppression in the form of a media blackout of any mention of Mandela's name or use of his picture. Neither was he allowed to have visitors. All the guards were white. Prisoners had to work in a quarry—a punishment that remained in effect for thirteen years. Winning the right to wear an individual uniform became an important victory in the fight for the prisoners' humanity on an island once set aside for lepers. Other reforms that Mandela and his fellow political prisoners won were the rights to use the courtyards on weekends and to play board games. Mandela began correspondence courses and studied for degrees in 1964. He opened lines of communication with the warden, which was difficult, but necessary. Communication with other groups of prisoners was also hard yet led to many ingenious successes. The dark years at Robben prison can be compared to the dark year of Mani. Like Mandela, Mahatma Gandhi also felt that prison could be helpful for one's spiritual development.

Mandela and the ANC leadership had some successes in dealing with fascist wardens, like Badenhorst, and with antagonistic prisoners, like Toivo, the leader of SWAP. Such successes encouraged them to form courses for their fellow political prisoners. Mandela and the other leaders tried to educate and inspire their fellow inmates. They called their effort "the university." The major fields of study were political science and economics—especially the history of the ANC and Marxist economics. Mandela, who was a lawyer, got to know his fellow prisoners better. They often asked for advice about their cases, and Mandela often ended up taking on their appeal cases.

Mandela's decision to write his autobiography was discussed earlier. It formed the counterpoint to the University—not the truth in a field of knowledge, but the truth of an individual's long walk to freedom. Mandela had had to avoid attempts on his life from the beginning of his stay on Robben Island. He realized that the authorities could arrange a plan of escape for him and try to use his desire for freedom against him. He recounted how the complicated and clever plans to assassinate him were foiled. Since Mandela and his colleagues continued to insist on being treated as human beings, the warden continued making concessions. By the 1970s prisoners simply held conversations at the quarry rather than engage in meaningless hammering. During this period of Mandela's life, he won the warden's approval to allow the prisoners to have hobbies. Mandela himself took up gardening and tennis. Mandela believed in the importance of meaningful manual labor and exercise for his health. He came to realize that gardening could even lead one to the insight that the daily life itself is sacred.

By the late 1970s Mandela's influence on the prisoners on Robben Island began to expand. A new generation of black youth had rebelled against the South African regime because of the massacre in Soweto in 1976. Many members of the South African Students' Organization, led by Patrick "Terror" Lakota, were sentenced to Robben Island. They caused the guards great difficulty. Mandela worked with their leader, Terror, and helped find unity between the ANC position and that of the Black Consciousness Movement of which Terror's group was a part. The "Terror" of the soccer field was able to enter the dialectical thought of Mandela and see how it led to a true synthesis and brought their opposing positions into a higher unity. Mandela's success as a unifier behind the prison walls soon became the cornerstone for the new strategy devised by Oliver Tambo and the ANC exile leadership. Mandela became the focus of the protest directed against the apartheid regime. The slogan "Free Mandela" became an international organizing tool. Mandela had just won the Jawaharlal Nehru Human Rights Award in India in 1979. Excluding his pictures and his writings from the news did not eliminate him from the public consciousness. He was almost elected to the honorific post of chancellor of the University of London.

In the following year, the South African authorities decided to move three members of the High Command of ANC, along with Nelson Mandela, to Pollmoor Prison. They were then isolated from the general population in an obvious effort to prevent Mandela from gaining the kind of influence that he had had at Robben Island. Instead of the repressive conditions they had endured, spacious and clean accommodations greeted them on the top floor of the prison. Mandela cultivated a large garden and gave away a large portion of his vegetables to other prisoners and to the wardens. He also became aware of the burgeoning growth of grassroots political organizations. They had firm links to the ANC, especially through the United Democratic Front which had named Mandela as its patron. The UDF united over six hundred anti-apartheid organizations. When Bishop Desmond Tutu won the Nobel Peace Prize in 1984, nations across the globe began to impose economic sanctions on Pretoria.

Feelers went out from the apartheid government of Botha to the leadership of the ANC to engage in discussions. When

Mandela was given a separate cell in 1985, he made the difficult decision to negotiate on his own. He recognized that such a path could lead to the appearance of compromising the democratic ideals that the Freedom Charter upheld, but the possibility of avoiding a race war convinced him to take it. After being properly dressed for the occasion, Mandela attended the first meeting with the government in May of 1988. The ANC leadership had been informed about meeting, and if not with unanimity, at least with consensus, it had permitted the discussions to go forward. When F.W. de Klerk took over for Botha in 1989, Mandela sensed that the government had begun to accept the need for negotiations. F.W. de Klerk freed Walter Sisulu and seven other leaders. The following year he freed Mandela and lifted the ban on ANC's political activity. Neither Mandela nor the ANC trusted de Klerk since he was also helping the Inkatha, a Zulu organization, attack the ANC by arming and transporting Zulu fighters. This attempt to weaken the ANC by the use of a "third force" mostly confused foreign observers with a white supremist bias who tended to think that black people would fight each other anyway.

Oliver Tambo returned from exile to join the newly freed leaders of ANC in December 1990. They worked with the leadership of UDF and the Congress of South African Trade Unions (COSATU) to form the convention for a Democratic South Africa (CODESA). CODESA began in December of 1991, fell apart due to government bribery and murders, and resumed in May. Even an Inkatha massacre of forty-six ANC supporters, the fourth mass killing that week, could not derail CODESA II. A democratic national election was set for April 27, 1994. When twenty million people went to the polls, they gave the ANC a plurality of 62% and a major voice in forming a ruling coalition. Mandela had won the Nobel Peace Prize jointly with DeKlerk the previous year. He now had the task of forming a new government, the result of the country's first national, nonracial, one-person-one-vote election. The election victory in 1994 actually provided Mandela with a chance to lead a "unity" government that would last for five years. In 1999 a government would then be elected that would reflect the will of the people through political parties in the fashion of other parliamentary democracies. Mandela's real task—in the words Lincoln once used to describe the healing needed after the American Civil War—was to bind up the nation's wounds.

Mandela could not have achieved the kind of success that he had had in prison without the firm support and hard work of his fellow ANC colleagues and comrades. When he was released from prison in 1990, Mandela discovered a whole new generation of ANC organizers and leaders who had renewed the anti-apartheid movement in his absence. In *Township Politics*, one of these activist-organizers, Mzwanele Mayekiso, explained how he and other ANC members formed the Alexandra Action Committee in 1985. In response to Tambo's call in January of that year to make South Africa ungovernable, the AAC began forming what they called "civics" in a slum of Johannesburg. In an area of about two square miles in which about 350,000 people lived in wretched conditions, Mayekiso and his fellow leaders of the AAC tried to protect Johannesburg's poorest and most destitute people from urban removal.

The problems facing the AAC in 1986 included crumbling roads, a lack of public transportation, shack housing, a lack of water and electricity, rampant crime, inadequate education, and the absence of health care. Mayekiso helped form the seeds for the future organs of people's power. He and four other ANC leaders established yard committees on ten major streets in an attempt to serve over 200,000 people. These committees first took on a task of lowering the crime rate. They established people's courts (which were comparable to those in the Paris Commune) and replaced the school's curriculum with new classes (which could be compared to "the University" at Robben Island). They worked out concrete ways of solving the myriad other difficulties that faced Alexandra by involving the members of the yard committees in improving their own community, as impoverished as it might be. The success of the anti-crime campaign was so dramatic that the streets became safe. By early 1986, women could walk alone, and workers never worried about being mugged.

As similar successes filled the people with hope for the future, the South African authorities brought down a reign of terror. Agent provocateurs tried to disrupt the committees' work, assassins murdered ANC leaders, gangs were allowed by the police to harass and extort residents, and the Inkatha were armed and protected by police when they massacred civilians attending ANC meetings and gatherings. Since those tactics did not stop Mayekiso and his fellow leaders, the police arrested them for treason and held them in prison for over two years until their trial in 1989. Mayekiso and others accused of treason were punished with solitary confinement, torture, and not being given medical attention or seeing a doctor. The food was mostly inedible, and hunger strikes seemed an appropriate response. Deaths occurred due to "slipping on a bar of soap" and then falling out of an eighth-floor window.

Mayekiso and the leaders of AAC responded to imprisonment much as Mandela had done. Each prison cell elected a committee of four persons to lead the study groups, cleanup, and meet their cultural needs—for example, celebrating Mandela's birthday on July 18th. The real goal was to transform each cell, containing thirty-eight people each, into a home. With three cells to a floor and four of the six floors containing political prisoners, another "University" arose. The warden responded by sending in agent provocateurs to spy and cause dissension. The activists found out who many of them were and even managed to turn some of them into supporters. The constant harassment by the guards did take its toll, however, causing some prisoners to attempt suicide and others to give up participating in the struggle. For those able to withstand such fascist repression, the transformation from street activists into political thinkers became a reality.

The trial of the Alexandra Action Committee leadership (minus two activists who had managed to go underground) began in 1987. Like Mandela's trial, the South African courts expected to get rid of Mayekiso and the four other leaders with a guilty verdict and spared no expense bringing in witnesses and evidence over the two-year period that the trial lasted. Because of Moses Mayekiso's (Mzwanele Mayekiso's older brother) strong connection with the South African metalworkers' union, he could gather union support, even that of the UAW union. Such support led to publicity and international interest in this trial. The ACC leadership worked with its legal team to try to present in a truthful way the actual goals and practice of the people's courts and the yard committee system. As the witnesses paraded through the court room, they often just told the truth and even expressed appreciation for the incredible gift that their community organizers had blessed them with—the chance to become independent and decide for themselves what served their interest. The Supreme Court judge who heard the case ruled in favor of the defendants, showing that their decision to tell the truth had brought them freedom.

When they returned to the streets of Johannesburg, the AAC leaders planned to launch a new civic by December of 1989. They could not stay in Alexandra at night due to the danger of assassination. Despite such difficulty they did organize an "Affordable Housing for All" Campaign in June. The repression resumed, however, and the inevitable arrest came at the end of November. Mayekiso went on a three-week hunger strike until his release. The authorities would attack civics, arrest their leaders, and try to prevent the seeds of the organs of people's power from growing. The question of whether mass-democratic, independent, and non-party political organs for poor and working people could emerge as permanent forces and play a real role in society was still be be answered.

With Mandela's return to South African society in 1990, the renewal of the civic in Alexandra was put on hold. Other initiatives of the ANC leadership began to take precedence. People who had been marginalized by apartheid laws now needed to take part in a national election and vote. Even with the historic victory at the polls in 1994—in fact, because of it—an even greater drain on the civics occurred. The best organizers and leaders, along with the most intelligent researchers and specialists in the movement, were co-opted into government jobs and served on government commissions.

If the previous two chapters are now compared with this chapter, certain similarities among Mahatma Gandhi, Martin Luther King, Jr., and Nelson Mandela can arise. Chart L attempts to summarize the beliefs and achievements that they have in common.

The research on the possible past lives of Mahatma Gandhi and Reverend Dr. King suggested that they may have worked together in the ninth century as Parzival and Sir Gawain. The research done by W.J. Stein indicated that a third character in *Parzival* played an equally important role—Feirefiz, the half-brother of Parzival and the leader of the Muslim army. While much less was told about the life and character of Feirefiz, he too came to the Grail and received the tidings of the Kingdom of God entering mankind. He then took up the mission to bring this truth back to the East and to unite it with the Eastern religions.

CHART L

A Comparison of the Three Pillars of the Social Movements for Nonviolence and Truth in the Twentieth Century

		MOHANDAS GANDHI	MARTIN LUTHER KING, JR.	NELSON MANDELA
TRUTH IN TESTIMONY	1.	Speech to the court in 1922	"Letter from Birmingham Jail"	Speech to the court in 1964
AUTO-BIOGRAPHY	2.	*The Story of My Experiments With Truth*	"Pilgrimage to Nonviolence"	*Long Walk to Freedom*
UNITY OF RELIGIONS	3.	Hinduism, Islam, and Christianity in Tolstoy Farm	"I Have a Dream"	Freedom Charter
SERVICE TO COMMUNITY	4.	Natal Indian Congress	Souther Christian Leadership Conf.	African National Congress
NOBEL PEACE PRIZE	5.	(no award - 1948)	1964	1993
HELPING THE OPPRESSED	6.	indentured servants and Untouchables	ending segregation of Jim Crow laws	ending apartheid
ORGANIZING COMMUNITY	7.	Satyagraha Ashram	Student Nonviolent Coordinating Com.	civics of AAC
GREAT COMMISSION	8.	India's independence	Poor Peoples Campaign	democratic elections in South Africa

A comparison of the three leaders of the nonviolent social movements in the twentieth century may reveal that the three pillars of the ideal human being in *Parzival* could collaborate from afar, as it were, to inspire poor and oppressed people on three different continents a millennium later. Gandhi began his activity by founding the Natal Indian Congress in South Africa in 1894. His development of a grassroots organization dedicated to helping coolies overcome their oppression was so successful that in 1912 John Dube founded the African National Congress based on the same principles and beliefs and using the same organizational methods as the NIC. The ANC became the vehicle for Mandela to enter the struggle for freedom. It contained the golden tradition of Gandhism that he could re-enliven and raise to a higher level. When Gandhi left South Africa and returned to India in 1915, he founded the Satyagraha Ashram, his new vehicle, and took on the mission of bringing India its independence from the British Empire. For thirty-three years he devoted himself to this goal. Shortly after achieving it in 1948, he was gunned down by an assassin. Gandhi's influence continued beyond his death and helped inspire Dr. King when he took on the leadership of the Montgomery bus boycott in 1955. Dr. King had learned about nonviolence when studying the theology of Niebuhr in Divinity School. He applied Gandhi's ideas during the boycott. His autobiography, "Pilgrimage to Nonviolence," shows the deepening of Gandhi's influence in the following decade of Dr. King's life.

Mandela experienced Gandhism in a different way than had Dr. King. He felt its influence very strongly when he became a member of the ANC and renewed its activity by founding the Youth League of ANC. He even met Gandhi's eldest son, the leader of the Natal Indian Congress, and worked with him to protest the original apartheid laws in 1950. The insight he gained by studying these laws and related ones, however, convinced him that a police state was coming. Mandela believed that renouncing violence would make protests impossible, that they would become like Sharpeville, simply massacres. In forming the Spear of the Nation, he chose to protect the ANC as a separate organization by carrying out acts of sabotage in retaliation for the violence the police state inflicted on the ANC and its supporters. He realized that his actions moved him outside of the realm of Gandhism and nonviolence. He was genuinely shocked when he was informed that he was a recipient of the Nobel Peace Prize. Other people did understand Mandela's actions and saw that they were taken for the cause of peace and brotherhood.

On Election Day in 1994, Mandela brought the influence of Gandhi in South Africa full circle. Thirty-three years after founding Umkhonto we Sizwe (the Spear of the Nation), Mandela voted in the election that brought democracy to South Africa. Mandela travelled to Natal to cast his ballot in the polling place nearest to the grave of John Dube, the first president of the ANC. He knew he was fighting for a cause that so many wonderful friends and heroes had sacrificed their lives for. A century after Mahatma Gandhi had founded the NIC, Nelson Mandela voted for the ANC in the first vote of his entire life. Chart M attempts to summarize this interrelation among the three nonviolent social movements of the twentieth century.

CHART M

A Timeline of the Nonviolent Social Movements in the Twentieth Century

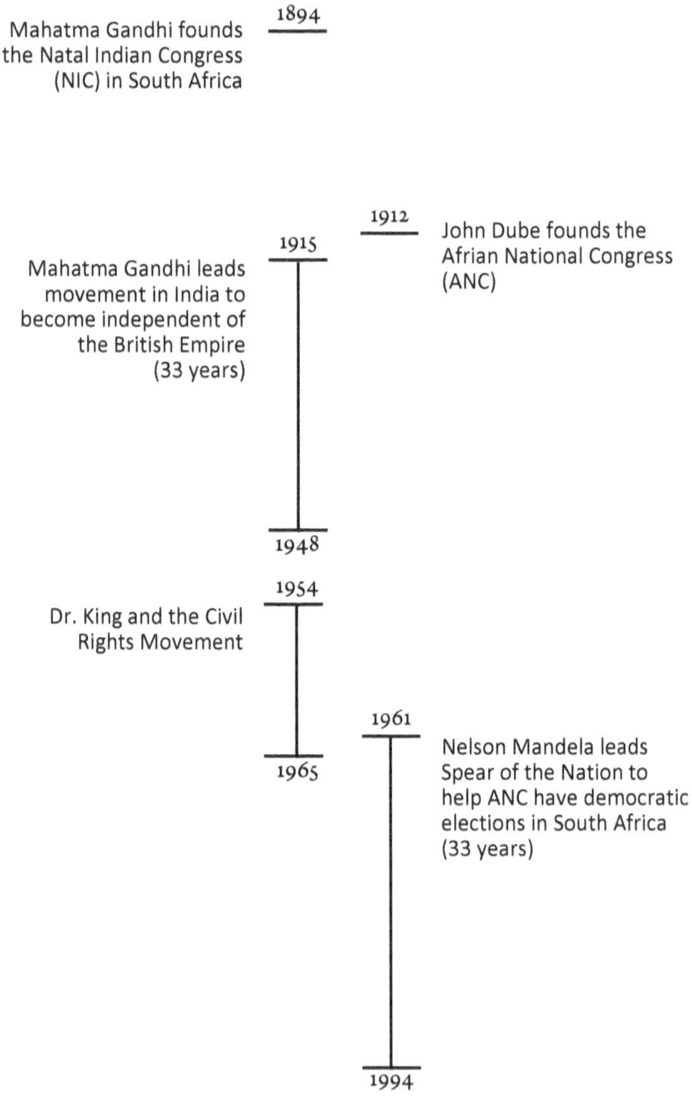

Mahatma Gandhi founds the Natal Indian Congress (NIC) in South Africa — 1894

1912 — John Dube founds the Afrian National Congress (ANC)

Mahatma Gandhi leads movement in India to become independent of the British Empire (33 years) — 1915 to 1948

Dr. King and the Civil Rights Movement — 1954 to 1965

1961 — Nelson Mandela leads Spear of the Nation to help ANC have democratic elections in South Africa (33 years) — to 1994

7.
El-Hajj Malik El-Shabazz (Malcolm X) and the Black Power Movement

Malcolm X began working on his autobiography by meeting with Alex Haley, who had taken on the task of writing up an "as told to" book for Ballantine, a publishing house in New York. Elijah Muhammad had given approval for the project of Malcolm X; otherwise Malcolm would not have told his life story for publication. From the summer of 1963 until his death on February 21, 1965, Malcolm met with Alex Haley, discussed the events of his life, edited what Haley had written up, and updated him on the momentous changes that had began occurring in his worldview due to his suspension and expulsion from the Nation of Islam and his attempt to form a new organization. Alex Haley was quite adamant about not letting Malcolm rewrite the earlier events in his life when he had extolled The Honorable Elijah Muhammad. The change in Malcolm's world outlook that occurred during his pilgrimage to Mecca is filled with the same Spirit of Truth that had inspired Gandhi's autobiography.

Malcolm Little was born on May 19, 1925. His father, Earl, was a follower of Marcus Garvey and thus an enemy of the Black Legion, a white supremacist group in Lansing, Michigan. Malcolm's earliest memory is from 1929 when Black Legionnaires attacked his house and set it on fire. He recalled that his mother, Louisa, and his four brothers and sisters barely escaped the flames. When the police and firemen arrived, they just watched it burn to the ground. The Little family moved to East Lansing where Earl Little was murdered in 1931. Malcolm remembered Louise having a vision of Earl's death and trying to warn him but to no avail. The police did not investigate Earl's assassination, and the life insurance company pretended that Earl had bashed in his own skull and then laid down on the streetcar tracks to be run over. Louisa had to become the breadwinner, but the strain of earning money, caring for a family, and being harassed by welfare workers proved to be too much. She was committed to the State Mental Hospital in Kalamazoo in 1937. Malcolm believed that the state social service agency had destroyed his family.

While Malcolm did not adjust well to being in a foster home as a ward of the state, he did get along well with Mrs. Swerlin, the head of the reform school where he was sent in 1938. That fall he entered the Mason Junior High and became so popular that he was elected president of his seventh-grade class. Looking back on this part of his life, Malcolm realized that the kindness of his white classmates was that of the affection they felt toward a mascot. This truth was brought home in eighth grade when a teacher he looked up to, Mr. Ostrowski, discouraged Malcolm's desire to become a lawyer. The consequence of the double life he was leading meant that he was expected to know his place and not try to become anything more that a menial worker. When Malcolm realized the full meaning of "uppity," he lost all interest in education. When he visited his half-sister, Ella, in Roxbury, he saw churches, music, and black society in a new way. With the change occurring in Malcolm's worldview, entering into the Harlem of Boston seemed to offer him deliverance from the *de facto* segregation of the North. Somehow Ella pulled sufficient strings for Malcom's custody to be transferred to her in Boston.

Malcolm arrived in Boston in the summer of 1941 at sixteen years of age. With the help of Shorty, a homeboy from Lansing, he landed a job as a shoeshine boy at the Roseland State Ballroom. He got his first conk, bought a zoot suit, and learned lindy-hopping. He began his descent into what he later called his self-degradation. What he regretted the most was how his wild ways affected his girl friend, Laura. His betrayal of her by taking up with Sophia led to Laura's self-destruction. At age seventeen, Malcolm moved to New York City and became what he called a "Harlemite," a hustler making money selling reefer. Malcolm went by the name of Detroit Red. The following year he returned to Boston, lucky to have survived and so wasted by his overuse of drugs that he spent a month at Shorty's trying to recover. His next hustle was to get Shorty, Sophia, her sister, and a friend named Rudy to form a burglary ring. His cleverness was remarkable, but a complete lack of common sense doomed their project from the onset.

When Malcolm was caught, he and Shorty received eight-to-ten-year prison sentences while Sophia and her sister received one-to-five-year sentences at a reformatory. In some strange way the good luck that had protected Malcolm from certain death in New York seemed active again right before he turned twenty-one. In Charlestown prison Malcolm underwent a further change. Rather than conning people and reveling in drugs and women, Malcolm chose to withdraw from people and live in darkness. He spent most of his two years at Charlestown in solitary confinement. He preferred isolation to talking to his follow inmates who ended up calling Malcolm by the name of Satan. The one prisoner who struck Malcolm positively was Bimbi. Under his influence Malcolm enrolled in correspondence courses.

When Malcolm was transferred to Concord Prison in 1948, another change in character occurred. His younger brother, Reginald, wrote him a letter and told him to stop eating pork and to quit smoking. Thinking Reginald had some kind of con game arranged for his escape, Malcolm followed his advice. Later that year Ella's efforts paid off, and Malcolm was transferred to a different prison. Norfolk Prison Colony was an experimental prison based on the idea of rehabilitation and funded by a philanthropist. It had classrooms, a huge library, and no bars on the windows. Reginald visited Malcolm and told him about the Nation of Islam and their beliefs. Malcolm compared his experience of Reginald's visit to the conversion of St. Paul at Damascus. The truth of his years of self-degradation struck him down with guilt. Only through his own efforts at self-education could he hope to rise up a new man.

The recollection of most people who read Malcolm's autobiography centers on his learning to read and write by studying the dictionary after "lights out" and becoming a masterful speaker by joining the prison debate club. The benefits of prison for someone who wants to undertake self-development are enormous. Another event occurred at this time that is difficult to understand but which proved decisive in convincing Malcom to follow Reginald's suggestion and to fall under the sway of Elijah Muhammad. It involved receiving a visit from Master W.D. Fard, which was physically impossible since he would have had to walk through concrete to visit Malcolm in his room late at night. Since Malcolm had no knowledge of occult powers and no interest in studying them, he did not suspect their misuse nor the reason for Fard's deception.

Malcolm did have trouble accepting the suspension of Reginald from the Nation of Islam. A personal letter from Elijah Muhammad helped Malcolm maintain his loyalty to the Nation of Islam and obedience to its highly restrictive and puritanical code of conduct. When he was released from prison in 1952, Malcolm joined the Detroit Temple and became Malcolm X. He began "fishing" for new members and travelled to Chicago to meet The Honorable Elijah Muhammad. His success in bringing in new converts led him to visiting Boston, Philadelphia, and New York. He achieved his largest increase in membership by fishing for Evangelicals. In the same year, 1954, he became Minister Malcolm X. When he received a car in 1956, his mission to expand the number of temples in America was made easier. By 1962 the number of mosques had increased from two to over one hundred. Malcolm X estimated that membership over that time span had increased from 400 to 40,000, which agrees with the estimates of scholars. These scholars tended to attribute this one-hundred-fold increase in membership to Malcolm X's power to command a room and to his talent for oratory. Whenever and where-ever he spoke, membership increased.

Malcolm's devotion to the cause was total and complete. An important change in his personal life, however, did occur in 1958. He married Betty X (later Betty Shabazz). Like Gandhi, his relationship with his wife suffered due to the traditional role that women were expected to take on in the Nation of Islam. Malcolm X had already shown his intolerance for the white devils. Now a similar intolerance expressed itself in his lack of trust in the woman who had borne him four children. Only leaving the Nation of Islam in 1964 would enable him to appreciate the nobility of all men, regardless of their color, and of all women, who ennoble family life through their humanity.

Malcolm helped to strengthen the Nation of Islam internally by founding a newspaper, *Muhammad Speaks*. This weekly newspaper informed members of important activities around the country and provided a platform for Muhammad to clarify his beliefs. He also strengthened the Nation of Islam externally by taking a trip to Africa in 1959 to internationalize the struggle. The American media had to take notice. The television program, "The Hate That Hate Produced," coupled with a book, *The Black Muslims in America*, raised the issue of the Nation of Islam to national prominence. Large-scale rallies attracted a black-only audience of thousands who came to hear Elijah Muhammad speak. The Federal Bureau of

Investigation and its director, J. Edgar Hoover, also took note and initiated wiretapping phones and sending in agent provocateurs. Some of these informants admitted to Malcolm who they were and joined the Nation of Islam due to a sincere change of heart.

Malcom devoted more of his time to the college lecture circuit and perfected his delivery. He had spoken at over fifty colleges and universities by the summer of 1963. His own view of the source of his immense popularity was a gift that he possessed. It enabled him to sense the temperament of his audience. Malcolm X was not aware of how jealous Elijah Muhammad had became because of his success speaking with college-educated young people. The previous year in 1962, Herbert Muhammad, Elijah's son and the publisher of *Muhammad Speaks*, instructed the press to print as little as possible about Malcolm X. Due to the media's positive view of the March on Washington in 1963, Malcolm X felt that the Nation of Islam should take some kind of action. They needed to demonstrate their relevance to the burning social issues of the day. The separatist policy of the Nation of Islam extended to the ballot box. There would be no dancing, no smoking, no drinking, and no voting. Malcolm X was told not to speak out.

As part of the effort of the Nation of Islam to present a more positive image of itself in the American media, Malcolm X began working with Alex Haley on an article about the Nation of Islam in 1960. They also collaborated on a *Playboy* magazine interview in 1962. In the spring of 1963, Malcolm X was told of Elijah Muhammad's infidelities by his personal secretaries. In the summer he arranged with Alex Haley to write an 'As Told To' book which would become *The Autobiography of Malcolm X*. Malcolm began to suspect that he was being set up as a fall guy for Elijah's infidelity. It was difficult for him to even think such thoughts—his idolization of his mentor had advanced so far. The directive of Elijah Muhammad silencing Minister Malcolm X came directly after Malcolm commented that President Kennedy's assassination showed that "the chickens are coming home to roost." Malcolm found out that the order to assassinate him had been given. A friend who had been given the assignment to assassinate him but could not carry it out told him so. Malcolm believed that his loyalty was being tested: was he loyal to a man whom he thought to be divine or was he loyal to the truth? He had to examine his own life to pass through this soul trial successfully. Fortunately, the very book he was working on with Alex Haley could help him find his way. He began to see that his great weakness was a lack of an academic education. Such an education would have exposed the foolishness of Yacub and the white devils, while the truth of the evil of white supremacy might have been traced back to its actual source. His work on the autobiography also led him to grasp his most important strength—that he would not sell out, could not be bought off, and would fight to the very end to help poor black people overcome the evil of white supremacy.

Malcolm X's change in character occurred first in his thinking life. He began to think for himself. He sought out the very secretaries who had been isolated and heard from them the truth about Elijah Muhammad's immorality. They also told him Elijah Muhammad's actual view of Malcolm—that he was Elijah's greatest minister but that he was dangerous and that Malcolm would betray him. The man who had raised Malcolm from the dead, the man whom Malcolm had always consulted when any problem arose, had not only silenced him, but ordered him to be killed. Malcolm turned to Ella and asked her for advice about his desire to go on a pilgrimage to Mecca, the Hajj. Ella encouraged him, even offering to pay for his trip. Malcolm left in March of 1964 and returned a changed man in May. He now tried to overcome the racism that had so infected him and began to develop tolerance for human beings of a paler complexion.

Malcolm also discovered the truth about women. His wife, Betty, became his source of strength. Her unwavering loyalty to Malcolm kept the family, now with four children, together. She became his anchor, the source of the steadfastness that would see him through the challenge of building a new vision of how to oppose the racism that threatened America and the world. Malcolm learned about Sunni Islam on the Hajj as well. He formed the Muslim Mosque in an attempt to bring a more genuine form of Islam into being as an alternative to the caricature that Elijah Muhammad espoused. He changed his name as well so that the inner transformation could appear outwardly. Malcolm X became El-Hajj Malik El-Shabazz.

The organization that Malcolm wanted to create as a replacement for the Nation of Islam would be open to all faiths and bring his ideas and corporate programs into the community. The visits that Malcolm made to various African countries following the Hajj, and on another long trip in 1964 as well, showed Malcolm the need for this new organization to think internationally. The meeting that he had with foreign leaders in Africa led him to conclude that the Organization for African American Unity, as he would finally name it, must support Pan-Africanism. He also concluded, as Nelson Mandela had done, that black people must take on the leadership of the OAAU and that concrete programs that met the actual needs of poor black communities must be implemented. Progressive white groups were the key for the success of OAAU. They needed to become active in their own communities, as well as providing support for the OAAU.

What Malcolm did not accept from the African leaders whom he met were their offers to take jobs in their administrations and come to live in Africa. Since the three leaders who made such offers are generally viewed as revolutionaries—Gamal Nasser of the United Arab Republic, Kwame Nkrumah of Ghana, and Ben Bella of Algeria—the offers may have reflected their insight into the assassination that would occur early next year. More importantly, these offers showed the deep respect these heads-of-state had for the talents and leadership ability of Malcolm. Rather than avoid the difficulties that a truth-speaker like Malcolm would bring in his trail, these three heads of state embraced them. They saw that the struggle for justice would benefit and that all of humanity would gain from the kind of society that Malcolm hoped to build.

CHAPTER 7   163

While Malcolm X was a member and minister of the Nation of Islam, he obeyed its rigorous code of conduct and believed in Elijah Muhammad's teachings. The one area where he tended to disagree with the Honorable Elijah Muhammad was in the failure of the Nation of Islam to take a stand on social issues like the Civil Rights groups had done. His lack of experience with, or understanding of, secret societies condemned him to be duped by one of them. There are religious secret societies, like the Society of Jesus and the Mormons, there are secular ones, like the Freemasonic Lodges and Scientology, and there are politically oriented ones like the Black Legion and Skull and Bones. The Nation of Islam is a religious one, and its actual founder was W.D. Fard, a man who convinced Elijah Poole (Elijah Muhammad's given name) that he—Fard—was actually the Savior, called the Messiah, the Christ, or Madhi in the various religions. By controlling the uneducated Elijah, Fard could remain in control of the Nation of Islam without having to be seen.

The heart of a secret society is the secret doctrine that it possesses. Like the Ku Klux Klan and the Nazis, the Nation of Islam presented to its members a twisted version of what is actually the prehistory of Atlantis and the creation of the five races. The white racist groups view the last race created as the superior one, while the black racist groups insist that the first race was superior. The truth is, as Jefferson indicated, that all men are created equal. In chapter two the past lives of Lincoln, (i.e. Hamlet, Hannibal, and Hector), showed that a pillar of the Temple of Liberty can incarnate in different races and still be the same noble man. The myth of Yacub that Fard created is a transparent fabrication. The idea that an ancient precursor of Gregor Mendel could have created the races of mankind in the service of white supremacy is scientific fantasy. Since Fard wanted materialistic followers, he also denied the truth about life after death and the spiritual world in general. For uneducated people kept away from white people by Jim Crow laws or *de facto* segregation to believe such a caricature is only possible if they become a cult and reinforce their belief by remaining separated. The counterpart of Fard's story—that black people like Frederick Douglass and Dr. King are inferior—is propagated by many Western secret societies and by the Ku Klux Klan in particular. Fard's actual goal was to inculcate in the black community a form of racism that would prevent what appeared in 1960 as the Civil Rights Movement from working toward the goal of the Blessed Community.

The refusal of educated people to believe in the activities of secret societies in religious, social, and political institutions is the other side of the susceptibility of the uneducated to become members of such cults. People who read *The Autobiography of Malcolm X* do not understand Malcolm's message if they fail to grasp the fact that the Nation of Islam is a secret society and that Fard stood behind it. The reason that Malcolm believed in Elijah Muhammad is because Malcolm underwent a conversion. In St. Paul's experience on the road to Damascus, Christ Jesus appeared to him in a vision. In Norfolk Prison Colony in 1949, Master W. D. Fard appeared to Malcolm in the form of a living human being. All doubt vanished, nor did

Malcolm ever think to do research on how occult powers can be misused. Such powers as astral projection would never be used to the detriment of human freedom by an initiate on the white path. Such an initiate would also never misuse knowledge of a person's past lives. Those educated people who insist that knowledge of where a certain person would be born is impossible should consider that Christianity began with such knowledge. When the three Magi followed the star to Bethlehem, they came bearing gifts. They refused to tell Herod where the birth occurred and warned Joseph and Mary to flee. Those who view reincarnation as a hoax might study Hinduism or even Christianity where Christ Jesus said that John the Baptist was the reborn Elijah. The lengths that Fard went to in order to bring Malcolm Little into the Nation of Islam suggest that he did know who he was. Elijah Muhammad even told some of his family and close friends that he knew Malcolm X would turn on him, knowledge that could have only come from Fard. In the meantime, Malcolm increased membership a hundredfold, founded over a hundred temples, and demonstrated his power to command a room.

The change in Malcolm's worldview in the final year of his life is in keeping with the previous changes that Malcolm went through in the earlier stages of his life. In his childhood the state of Michigan made him its ward by taking away his mother, sending her to a state mental health hospital, and placing him in a foster home. The twelve-year-old Malcolm became rebellious, and the following year was sent to reform school. He got along with the person in charge, Mrs. Sterling, and attended Mason Junior High. He was successful in his studies and popular with his classmates who elected him class president. He called this part of his life "Mascot" since he was the only black student at this school and was simply acting the role of the stereotypical good Negro. One of his teachers, Mr. Ostrowski, informed him of this reality when he answered Malcolm's question about becoming a lawyer by explaining that such a profession was not suitable for him. Malcolm had changed from rebellious to conforming to a stereotype, and now he was ready to change his character once again.

Malcolm's summer trip to visit Ella in Boston led him to move there the following summer and take a job as a shoeshine boy at the Roseland Ballroom. With homeboy Shorty's help, Malcolm changed from country hick to cool hipster, no longer the mascot who obediently played his part. Malcolm became the hustler who cheated everyone. By 1942 he graduated to Harlem and sold reefer. When he returned to Boston, he formed a burglary ring and was finally caught. In February 1946, three months before his twenty-first birthday, Malcolm was sentenced to eight-to-ten years in prison. He was so filled with hate that the other prisoners began to call him Satan. His anti-religious attitude turned him against everyone, even his fellow prisoners. Malcolm broke rules just so he could be punished with solitary confinement.

From "Satan," the opposite of the cool hipster, Malcolm changed again. Reginald introduced him to the Nation of Islam, and W.D. Fard magically appeared to him in prison. From being completely and empathically irreligious, Malcolm suddenly began following the stringent rules of a religious cult and believed in its secret doctrine. Malcolm himself called the change that he went though at age twenty-three a conversion. The chapter in Malcolm's autobiography following the one on Satan is entitled "Saved."

Upon his release from prison in 1952 after serving six years of his sentence, Malcolm devoted his life to representing the Nation of Islam and was elevated by Elijah Muhammad to the office of minister. Minister Malcolm X unleashed all of his considerable talent to the task of bringing new members into the Nation of Islam. His "fishing" increased membership one-hundredfold. After a decade of being Elijah Muhammad's minister of ministers, he entered another period of change. From reverent service as minister, he turned to the task of trying to think for himself about the weaknesses and errors that he had discovered in the man whom he had idolized. Problems arose in 1963, the most serious being that Elijah silenced him in November. The event that led Malcolm to find a solution occurred in February 1964 when he took a pilgrimage to Mecca. His discovery that the story of Yacub was a lie shook the beliefs of a man who had fought so vigorously and so long for the truth.

In his meetings with various white people on the pilgrimage, he experienced the depth of the lie of black racism that he had been taught. In his meetings with various world leaders, both during the time of this pilgrimage and later that summer, he began to imagine a future organization that he hoped to create. His ideas included black leadership, concrete programs to meet the needs of poor black people living in ghettoes, and an outreach program to unite with similar movements around the globe. Malcolm took the name El-Hajj Malik El-Shabazz. He saw that the difference between himself and most other leaders was his refusal to sell out the poor and oppressed whom he wished to serve. He had evolved from a Mascot, playing the role of the stereotypical good Negro, to the Hustler, cheating everyone around him, to Satan himself, filled with hate and completely irreligious, to the Saved, devoted to Islam and obeying a host of arbitrary rules, to a Minister, serving Elijah Muhammad and making the Nation of Islam the fastest growing black organization in America, to El-Hajj Malik El-Shabazz, the Revolutionary, willing to confront de facto segregation and racism in the urban areas of the North and refusing to sell out those he served.

Malcolm's death in the Audubon Ballroom on February 21, 1965, coincided with the collapse of his fledgling organization, the Organization of African American Unity. Just as Gandhianism could not survive without Mahatma Gandhi, neither could the OAAU without Malcolm X. What did survive and grow and flourish came about because of the project that Malcolm had undertaken in 1963 in collaboration with Alex Haley, *The Autobiography of Malcolm X*. In Malcolm's life, the Spirit of Truth triumphed. Because of his ruthless truthfulness about the reality of the earlier stages of his life, the simplicity and clarity of his final vision shone all the more brightly. For those black leaders who needed insight into the revolutionary potential that was present in the inner cities of

America, Malcolm had provided a blueprint. For white people who might be interested, a similar plan existed.

The publication of Malcolm's autobiography in 1965 led to an ever-widening circle of readers. For the white coed who had asked "What can I do?" Malcolm now provided an answer. One man in particular, Huey P. Newton, read Malcolm's book and decided to act upon his indications. He joined with Bobby Seale, and together they canvassed the poor black community in Oakland, California in 1966 and discovered its specific needs and devised programs to meet them. Later that year Huey Newton and Bobby Seale founded the Black Panther Party for Self-Defense. Its name is controversial, and most historians seem to imagine that Huey and Bobby were studying up on Civil Rights history one night and came across a progressive political party in the state of Mississippi and thought that its name would be a good choice for their new organization. It is more likely that Huey P. Newton read a page of the introduction to *The Autobiography of Malcolm X* and saw Malcolm's mannerisms described as those of a black panther. The ideal of self-defense, which was part of Huey's original vision, distinguished it from the nonviolent protests of Gandhi and Dr. King. Though it was later dropped from its name, it was emphasized in posters showing armed Black Panther Party members. Huey Newton expressed his view of the influence of Malcolm on the Black Panther in *Revolutionary Suicide*: "Therefore, the words on this page cannot convey the effect that Malcolm has had on the Black Panther Party, although, as far as I am concerned, it is the testament on his life's work."[15]

---

15 Huey Newton, *Revolutionary Suicide*, p.102.

The ten-point platform of the Black Panther Party (BPP) was the basis for providing the free breakfast-for-children programs and the free health clinics. The success of these programs extended beyond the communities they served. City schools soon had free lunch programs. The success of the free health clinic was so great that the leadership of the BPP ended up requiring each of its branches to implement one. Dr. Quentin Young worked with Fred Hampton and "Doc" Satchel to establish one in Chicago. He had worked with Dr. King and other Civil Rights leaders in Mississippi during Freedom Summer in 1964 as an active member of the Medical Committee for Human Rights. Four years later he helped establish the People's Medical Care Center in 1968 and visited it weekly. Some survival programs, as they were called, provided services not just for basic human needs, but for the specific needs of a poor black community. Such was the free busing-to-prison program that helped family members stay connected with their loved ones.

One of the controversial programs that the Panthers provided was community monitoring of police. The existence of police brutality has become a cause for major protests and demonstrations in the United States and around the world. Over fifty years ago the problem was worse. The Black Panther Party actually dealt with this problem in a practical way and helped the black community feel more secure and safe. Just as doctors, nurses, and interns volunteering their skills were necessary for the success of the peoples' clinics, so did lawyers have a key role to play in dealing with the harassment and intimidation that law enforcement agencies took part in.

All Black Panther Party members were required to sell the *Black Panther Party* newspaper, generally on street corners. The income from sales was a part of the financial plan to help fund the various programs and provide food and shelter for the cadre of full-time members. The party paper was also delivered to homes and stores. The idea of community-based organizing includes families and neighbors discussing the articles in the *Black Panther Party* newspaper and developing insights into how the problems of one's own hometown were solved in other cities and even other countries. Cadre were assigned the responsibility to work with the families along one or more blocks. Most importantly, the Panther newspaper was studied by the cadre, both individually and in study groups. It was a basic educational tool, along with other books, and served a purpose like that of Gandhi's weeklies—to uplift and to inspire free, creative thinking. The goal of community-based organizing was always to have members of the community speak for themselves about the issues in their community and to take on the leadership roles in the survival programs that emerged.

Huey Newton's leadership role lasted only for one year. His arrest for the shooting of a police officer, John Trey, on October 28, 1967, led to his imprisonment. The "Free Huey" movement helped to build support for the fledgling party. Almost three years passed before Huey was released, and much had happened. James Forman played an important role in the attempt to merge SNCC and the BPP together. The rise of Stokely Carmichael, later called Kwame Toure, to become the executive secretary of SNCC in 1966 was accompanied by the withdrawal of John Lewis and the implementation of

Malcolm X's idea of having an all-black organization to ensure that black leaders would actually make the decisions. SNCC's emphasis on community organizing made the idea of a merger with the BPP seem like a logical next step. SNCC leaders, like Stokely Carmichael and H. Rap Brown, did join the Panther leadership but failed to inspire more community members to serve the people, body and soul. James Forman withdrew from the Panther leadership but continued to be active in community-based organizing in Detroit. Stokely Carmichael and Rap Brown, who left later than Forman, seemed more interested in their image than building survival programs. When he returned, Huey Newton's plate was filled with disparate ideas and personality clashes. Hoping for leaders to emerge who would operate by consensus was the goal that Huey Newton sought. Clearly, his goal had not been reached, and Huey took charge and tried to bring about the new kind of leadership through study and education. He also attempted to internationalize the struggle by connecting with third world liberation groups as James Forman— in agreement with Malcolm's recommendations—had also advocated. By 1974, the threat of arrest—again on a murder charge—led Huey Newton to travel to Cuba to seek political asylum. When he returned in 1977, he was married. Many of his followers realized that his commitment to serving the people was no longer present. The disbanding of the Black Panther Party, now led by Elaine Brown, did not occur until a few years later.

Another look at Huey P. Newton's choice of his party's symbol may be fruitful. The three previous chapters each attempted to achieve a deeper insight into the lives of Gandhi, Dr. King, and Mandela by comparing them with the characters in *Parzival*: Parzival, Sir Gawain, and Feirefiz. If the question of the significance of the symbol of the black panther is raised in the context of Wolfram's epic about the Grail knights, one character stands out. Gahmuret, Parzival's father, had a black panther on his family's coat-of-arms. When Gahmuret changed his coat-of-arms to that of the Baruch Ahkarin, the anchor became his new crest of heraldry. It stood for steadfastness and faithfulness, the very qualities that Gamuret lacked. Gahmuret was faithless to his new wife and child, to Belacane and Feirefiz. Returning to Europe from Africa after his service to the leader of the cultural center of the world in Baghdad, Gahmuret changed his coat-of-arms back to the black panther. He again proved to lack steadfastness. He left his second marriage to Herzeleide and resumed fighting for the Baruch. Like Gahmuret, Huey Newton could not sustain his commitment to leading the party that he had founded. It may even seem ironic that a marriage is partly to blame for his lack of perseverance.

What Huey Newton could follow faithfully was not a cause—a high ideal—but rather a person, specifically Malcolm, the Revolutionary. Huey's embrace of Malcolm's idea of Black Power may be a reflection of the decision of Gahmuret to serve the man whom he viewed as the greatest leader in the world. Gahmuret did not object to Baruch Ahkarin's religion any more than Huey did to Malcolm's devotion to Islam. Huey Newton did look up to Malcolm as a great leader and saw the

Black Panther Party as a testament to his life. The emphasis on black leadership was Malcolm's, but the posters idealizing armed self-defense and the publicity surrounding armed Panthers entering the California legislature in Sacramento were all Huey's. The idea to build survival programs in the inner city was a further development of Malcolm's idea of having programs, like the one the Nation of Islam had established to help those suffering from drug addiction, that would meet the concrete needs of the poor people living in ghettoes. Huey's expansion of Malcolm's basic idea may even be seen in the light of Gahmuret's willingness to fight for and defend the "inner" army in the tournaments and the battles that he fought at Patelamunt and at Kanvoleis. In the twentieth century, Huey Newton fought for the inner city.

The possible past life of Malcolm Little (El-Hajj Malik El-Shabazz) as Baruch Ahkarin might be helpful in explaining how so many world leaders were willing to meet directly with Malcolm in 1964 and why three of them—Nasser of the United Arab Republic (Egypt), Nkrumah of Ghana, and Ben Bella of Algeria—offered him important positions in their administrations. The enormous show of respect that was given to Malcolm by so many world leaders, like that which would be granted to Mandela thirty years later, becomes more understandable if figures like the Baruch and Feirefiz stand behind them. (See chart N)

Malcolm X's success in recruiting new members for the Nation of Islam was mostly due to his speaking talent and ability to "read" his audience. Without Malcolm, the growth of the Nation of Islam would have been much slower. The role

CHART N

A Possible Past Life of Malcolm X (El-Hajj Malik El-Shabazz) and of Huey Newton

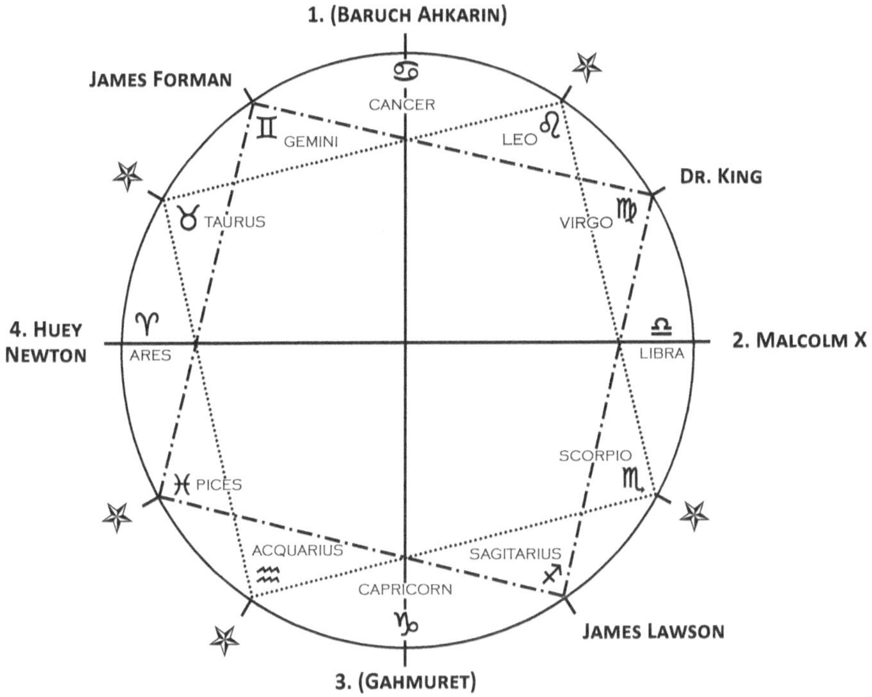

1. **BARUCH AHKARIN** moves from Cancer to Libra in three incarnations to become **2. MALCOLM X** and collaborate again in the House of Islam (the tone of naturalism or willing)

3. **GAHMURET** moves from Capricorn to Ares in three incarnations to become **4. HUEY NEWTON** and collaborate again with **BARUCH AHKARIN** and **MALCOLM X**.

that Fard played in Malcolm X's conversion and the warning that he gave Elijah Muhammad about Malcolm's eventual betrayal suggest that he knew full well about Malcolm's past lives. The unsuspected benefit of reading an autobiography is that the author generally gives a fairly clear picture of his or her worldview and world-soul-mood. Malcolm's worldview of realism is especially apparent in his loyalty. Without this soul quality, Malcolm's fervent devotion to The Honorable Elijah Muhammad could never have lasted as long as it did. His world-soul-mood is equally apparent in his oratorical talent which requires the use of coordinated (or dialectical) thinking. It also reveals itself in the reversals that characterize the seismic shifts that occurred in Malcolm's character development: from mascot to hustler to Satan to saved to minister, and finally to revolutionary.

The final change in Malcolm's character enabled him to envision working with Dr. King to expand the Civil Rights Movement to include organizing the poor and to internationalize the struggle for human rights by working with progressive groups around the world. Before his own death and three years after Malcolm's death, Dr. King went in exactly that direction. Malcolm was interested in preserving black leadership, but he was just as eager to unite with progressive white leaders. In this reversal of his views as Malcolm X, he may have been reflecting an appreciation for the great success that was brought him by having the white Christian Gahmuret join his military forces in the ninth century.

8.
Fred Hampton and the Rainbow Coalition

Fred Hampton was born in Argo, Illinois on August 30, 1948. His mother, Iberia, took care of him and his two older siblings until he was eight. She then got a job with Corn Products in 1956, and she became the union steward. Fred's family moved to Maywood in 1958, and Fred attended Proviso East High School from the fall of 1962 until he graduated with honors in the spring of 1966. Independently, Fred studied the writings of Marcus Garvey, W.E.B. DuBois, and Malcolm X. He also became interested in the NAACP. The president of the West Suburban chapter, Don Williams, encouraged Fred to take on the leadership of its youth chapter. In an impressive display of organizing ability, Fred increased the membership of a handful of young people to several hundred members in less than a year. He also set up a black cultural center in Maywood in 1966, the same year that Huey Newton and Bobby Seale were conducting a survey for the North Oakland Poverty Center that would become the basis for the ten-point program of the Black Panther Party.

Dr. Martin Luther King, Jr. came to Chicago in the summer of 1966 to bring nonviolent protests to the North. Fred was working a summer job at Corn Products to earn money for his college tuition. He was able to attend some of the marches for open housing in the company of Bill Taylor, the president of the union at Corn Products and a good friend of Iberia Hampton. Bill talked to Fred about the mounting violence that Dr. King was facing. In a change from his support for the marches, Fred met Dr. King and told him that his nonviolent tactics were useless against the rock-throwing racists in Marquette Park. Fred took another step in clarifying his viewpoint toward his country's racist heritage by refusing to register for the draft on his eighteenth birthday. In March of the following year, Dr. King returned to Chicago to give a speech on the Vietnam War that was more in tune with Fred's more radical viewpoint.

In the fall of 1967, Fred Hampton addressed a rally in Maywood and urged the participants to attend the Village Board meeting and protest the lack of activities and services for young black men. His speech landed Fred on the FBI's Key Agitator list, bringing him to the attention of J. Edgar Hoover. When SNCC opened an office in Chicago on 43rd Street the following March, Fred asked one of the leaders, Stokely Carmichael, to come to Maywood and speak to a rally that he had arranged. At this time, the central committee of the Black Panther Party was actively engaged in talks to bring SNCC, the Civil Rights group most active in community organizing, into a merger with the Black Panther Party.

Two other members of SNCC, Bobby Rush and Bob Brown, were impressed with Fred's introductory speech. Bobby Rush made contact with Fred Hampton following the riots that broke out in so many cities following Dr. King's assassination on April 4th. Fred and Bobby Rush began organizing in the summer of 1968 when the events surrounding the Democratic National Convention were capturing national attention. They arranged to purchase thousands of copies of the Black Panther Party newspaper and began selling them on street corners in the black community. A stream of income was generated which enabled them to begin to provide the necessities to the cadre who wanted to join them. The newspaper also provided an educational impulse to the community members who read it and to the cadre who studied and discussed its articles. Most importantly, it offered concrete examples of how to implement the Black Panther Party platform and its ten-point program.

In a completely unofficial capacity, Fred and Bobby began to open Free Breakfast-for-children sites in the black community, staffed by young black men and women and concerned parents. Fred Hampton and Ronald "Doc" Satchel met with Dr. Quentin Young in the Medical Committee for Human Rights headquarters where the Panthers also had an office. Whereas the Free Breakfast program could be run by community people, the Free Medical Care Centers did require doctors and other medical personnel to operate. Dr. Young's group had found progressive doctors who wished to provide medical care to the disadvantaged and had opened such clinics for the last several years in numerous cities often times in conjunction with the Black Panther Party.

The first concrete result of Fred Hampton landing on the FBI's Key Agitator list occurred in July of 1968 when he was charged by Ed Hanrahan with robbing an ice cream vendor.

This case was used to smear Fred Hampton's name and harass him. It also showed that just as free health clinics depend on the commitment of progressive doctors so did the leadership of the Black Panther Party require a similar commitment from progressive lawyers. Jeffery Haas and Dennis Cunningham first met one another while trying to help the various black men who had been rounded up in the wake of the riots that broke out after Dr. King's murder. Dennis became Fred's lawyer in October when he was introduced to him by a member of the Film Group which was planning a documentary on the Panthers. The plan for a movie on the Chicago Panthers thus preceded the official formation of the Black Panther Party Illinois chapter in November. The leadership of the Black Panther Party in Oakland took that step after meeting with Bobby Rush who had travelled to Oakland earlier that month to inform the Central Committee of the progress made in implementing their ten-point program.

Just as Fred had built up the Youth Chapter of the West Suburban NAACP so did he increase the membership of the Chicago chapter of the Black Panther Party until it became the largest one in the country. One major part of the membership was drawn from students. Fred gave lectures at the student unions of numerous colleges in the Chicago area. Following his lectures, he would stay and answer questions and inform the black students of ways that they could help the movement. Since many white students also attended his lectures, he would tell them that they should also stay, and that Slim Coleman would talk to them in another part of the auditorium or in another room. Another major part of the membership came from the churches in the black community. Fred became friends with a number of ministers and was invited to various church functions. That over half of the membership of the Black Panther Party in Chicago were women attested to the importance of the free breakfast programs, free after-school activity centers, a free health clinic, free busing to prisons for family members of prisoners, and community monitoring of police for the black women trying to raise a family in the "black belt", as the poorest, most segregated parts of Chicago were called. A third important part of the membership of the Black Panther Party in Chicago was made up of ex-servicemen like Bobby Rush himself. Army veterans returned from war to discover that the country that they had fought for was unwilling to correct the injustices of segregation. The Black Panther Party offered veterans a way to serve the ideals that founded this country by serving the people, body and soul.

Having won the Cook County States Attorney race in 1968, Ed Hanrahan took office in January 1969 and formed the Special Prosecution Unit to work with the Red Squad and the FBI who were keeping track of and sending in agent provocateurs to disrupt organizations that Hoover disapproved of. In June, Hanrahan also assembled a special unit of Chicago police officers led by Sergeant Groth and under Hanrahan's personal charge. On January 24th, Fred was arrested on an FBI tip by the Chicago police, but not handcuffed. He was then placed in the backseat of a police car where a gun just happened to be resting. Realizing he was being set up, he held his wrists out of the window and screamed about a gun being in the back seat. Thus, he avoided this first attempt of the FBI to murder him.

In February of 1969, Fred began working with other progressive groups in Chicago and formed the Rainbow Coalition. The Young Lords Organization, led by Jose "Cha Cha" Jimenez, had been a Puerto Rican gang which formed on the streets of Chicago in 1960. In 1968 they declared themselves to be a civil rights organization and fought to oppose the premeditated gentrification (then called Urban Renewal) that sought to drive them out of Lincoln Park as it had done to them previously in two other locations. Part of the success the Young Lords had experienced in their occupation of McCormick Theology Seminary, DePaul University, and Children's Memorial Hospital was due to the support of unions, the Independent Precinct Organization, Rising Up Angry, Concerned Citizens of Lincoln Park, and many more groups. Notably, a Methodist minister, Reverend Bruce Johnson, helped the Young Lords by letting them use his church—later named Peoples Church—as their headquarters. The murder of him and his wife in 1968 is still unsolved to this day. The murder of one of the leaders of the Young Lords Organization in April 1969 prompted Cha Cha Jimenez to take direct action by occupying the 18th district police station. The support the Young Lords received from the Puerto Rican community to carry out such a protest came about because of the survival programs, especially the free breakfast program and the free health clinic. Cha Cha Jimenez gave the credit to Fred Hampton: "Fred took the Young Lords under his wing. He gave us the skills that we needed to come right out of the gang and organize the community."[16]

Something similar occurred on the north side of Chicago in Uptown. Bobby Lee was chosen by Fred to meet with William Fesperman and the Young Patriot Organization. Bobby Lee's training sessions were tape-recorded, and those tapes are still available over fifty years later. They provide important insights into how to build survival programs and how such programs strengthen the community. Some Black Panther Party members disagreed with Fred's decision to form an alliance with a white group, especially since they commonly wore the Confederate flag. Fred felt that he had to form the Rainbow Coalition to clarify that the struggle was between the rich and the poor, and that poor whites must play an important role in the future, a role that must be prepared for. Fred Hampton used the Rainbow Coalition to show the black community that falling into the ideology of black nationalism and embracing black separatism, as the Nation of Islam had done, would lead to black capitalism and a perpetuation of exploiting the poor. Nelson Mandela experienced a similar problem when young organizers like "Terror" attacked the ANC for not supporting the Black Consciousness Movement.

Encouraging youth gangs in a Puerto Rican and a poor Appalachian community in Lincoln Park and Uptown to organize survival programs also helped deter crime in those

---

[16] "50 years of Fred Hampton's Rainbow Coalition," *South Side Weekly*, 9/27/2019, Chicago.

areas. Mzwanela Mayekiso watched Alexandra change into an area of safety by organizing "civics." Hampton tried to take the "bull by the horns," as it were, and arranged talks with the leaders of the two black gangs on Chicago's Southside. In May of 1969, Fred met with David Barksdale of the Devil's Disciples and negotiated a peace treaty which allowed the Panthers to sell their newspaper in Disciple's territory. He tried to get David to stop poisoning the black community with drugs and to join with the Panthers in serving the people, body and soul. But at least it was a start. State's attorney Ed Hanrahan was upset enough that he joined with Mayor Daley in officially declaring "A War on Gangs." Since the police viewed the Black Panther Party as a gang and the FBI's plan required its destabilization, twenty-eight members of the party were killed by police nationwide during 1969—including Fred.

The success of Chairman Fred, as he was commonly called, was not repeated in his meeting with the leader of the Blackstone Rangers, Jeff Fort. Not only was he almost gunned down by the Rangers before the meeting had begun, but the FBI tipped off the Chicago police that the Panthers were carrying weapons and the Chicago Police Department arrested them when they left the meeting. Jeff Fort wanted nothing to do with helping his community, but he did offer the Panthers a cut of the profit if they would sell drugs. Jeff Fort was strictly an opportunist, but the People's Law Office and Jeffery Haas later discovered that Marlin Johnson, the Special-Agent-in-Charge of the Chicago branch of the FBI, had given Fort an anonymous warning that the Panthers planned to kill him. The agent provocateur who had infiltrated the Black Panther Party had also told SAC Johnson that the Panthers were armed, which explained the FBI tip that got them arrested. In June Chairman Fred was brought to trial in Maywood and convicted of stealing seventy-one ice cream bars. Jeffery Haas, Fred's lawyer, showed the crookedness of the judicial system. He even found out who had actually robbed the vendor but not until some years later. Many civic leaders testified in Fred Hampton's defense that robbery was totally out of character for him, but the fix was in. The harassment unfortunately put Fred behind bars. Without his leadership, Bobby Rush realized that the flood of new members could not be incorporated into the Black Panther Party properly. He put a halt to accepting new members. The FBI saw an opportunity to use another agent provocateur to sow further chaos in the Black Panther Party. They sent George Sams to the Panther's office on West Madison Street. A couple of days later SAC Johnson led a task force to raid the office on the pretext that they were looking for Sams, a wanted fugitive. They took the money, the membership lists, and all other relevant information, and then the FBI agents trashed the office. Such attacks scared some Panther members, and they left the Black Panther Party.

The People's Law Office was formally organized as a law collective in the summer of 1969. Their clients included the Black Panther Party, the Young Lords Organization, the Young Patriots Organization, and Rising Up Angry. Skip Andrew, Donald Stang, Dennis Cunningham, and Jeffrey Haas were incredibly busy defending the leaders of the Rainbow

Coalition. In his book *The Assassination of Fred Hampton*, Jeffrey Haas credited the influence of Fred Hampton with bringing the members of the Peoples' Law Office together and inspiring them to pursue the legal case of the Hampton and Clark families to victory in 1982. Jeff Haas got Fred out on an appeal bond in 1969 for his conviction in the ice cream bar robbery. He attended Fred's speech that night at a church on Ashland Avenue and heard "I Am a Revolutionary." Fred had listened to tapes of Jesse Jackson's "I Am Somebody" and used its form, but its content was steeped in the Spirit of Truth. Dr. King's last speech in Memphis was also similar to Fred's speech, in that its content was filled with the knowledge of his coming death. Such knowledge of the future transforms the listener. By hearing Fred's words, Jeff Haas became inspired by the Spirit of Truth, and he and the People's Law Office would discover a way to bring the truth of Fred's assassination to the light of day.

Fred's speech was different from Martin Luther King's "I've Been to the Mountain Top" because Fred learned of his death more than three months before it occurred. He learned of it even before he had reached the age of twenty-one. Those who have read Malcolm X's autobiography cannot but agree with Ossie Davis's conclusion that Malcolm spoke truthfully, and that this ability distinguished him. Like Fred Hampton, Malcolm had to live with the knowledge of his coming demise for months. When Fred did turn twenty-one and others could see the writing on the wall, a meeting was held, and the possibility of Fred Hampton and Bobby Rush going underground was discussed. Unlike the leadership of ANC—who had no real knowledge of how to live underground or of an underground network—some of the people at Fred's meeting had such knowledge and experience. Fred Hampton did understand that he and Bobby were being offered a real alternative, but not a choice that would allow him to serve the people. Following Fred's death, this alternative was used by Cha Cha Jimenez when he went underground. Fred's decision to stay on as the chairman of the Chicago chapter of the Black Panther Party meant an early death, but his inspiration lived on even to the point that his fellow Panthers and supporters gathered for a year-long series of events celebrating each of the survival programs in turn leading up to a celebration of the fiftieth anniversary of his death.

Bobby Rush narrowly escaped death in that early morning hour of December 4th. He went to Fred's apartment on a daily basis and would have stayed there that night except for a family problem at home. One of the survivors of the raid said he heard a policeman say, "Bobby is next." Bobby Rush testified in court in 1977 as a witness for the Hampton and Clark families who were suing the FBI and the Chicago Police Department—twenty-eight defendants in all. When asked to characterize Fred Hampton, Bobby Rush said, "Fred was the motivating force inside the party. [He had] the dedication of a Malcolm X, the speaking ability of Martin Luther King and as far as courage, there are few with that type of courage."[17] He also told of the

---

17 Jeffrey Haas, *The Assassination of Fred Hampton*. Chicago: Lawrence Hill Books, 2009. pp.283-284

Panthers organizing poor people. On an ordinary Panther day, members would get up at 5:30 a.m., go to one of six Breakfast-for-Children sites, prepare and serve breakfast to the children, and then clean up. Members would spend their day selling Panther newspapers, soliciting contributions—including the food for the breakfast programs—or working in the office. After eating a communal dinner at Panther headquarters, they often had political education classes. The party provided money for food and rent out of contributions and speaking honoraria while friendly doctors provided free medical care.

Elaine Brown, the leader of the national Black Panther Party in 1977, also testified. She had travelled to Chicago in 1969 and was impressed by Fred Hampton then. In November of that year, the central committee of the Black Panther Party invited Fred Hampton to come to the West Coast to meet with the national leadership. When he arrived, Elaine met him and asked him if he would mind taking her place and speaking to a group of three hundred UCLA law students. She was overwhelmed by the power of his words and considered him to be the best speaker she had ever heard. She hoped that he would become the national spokesman of the party. When Fred met with the central committee, he was invited to become a member. Fred agreed, but he told the leadership that he wold continue to live in Chicago and lead the Chicago chapter.

In *The Assassination of Fred Hampton*, Haas reveals important facts about the conspiracy that led to the state-sponsored murder of Fred. The attack on Fred's apartment at 4:00 A.M.

on December 4, 1969, by fourteen Chicago policemen was led by Sergeant Groth who was under Hanrahan's command. The court trial revealed that the layout of the apartment had been drawn by the Panther's chief of security, William O'Neal, who was an agent provocateur working for the FBI. O'Neal gave the drawing of the layout to his handler, Roy Mitchell, who was an FBI agent. Mitchell then passed it on to a Hanrahan assistant, Robert Piper, and assured him that Fred Hampton would be in the apartment the night of December 3rd. Mitchell also instructed O'Neal to give Fred Hampton a powerful sedatives so that Fred could not resist when the police arrived. William O'Neal left 2337 W. Monroe early in the evening so that he would miss the policeman from Hanrahan's Special Prosecution Unit (SPU). The Federal Bureau of Investigation appreciated how O'Neal's help had made the raid a success. The week after the raid, Robert Piper asked for and received a special bonus to give to O'Neal who was being paid one hundred dollars per week by the FBI. William O'Neal had always refused to acknowledge his role in Fred's death until Eyes on the Prize interviewed him some twenty years later. Shortly after his admission, he returned to his home in Maywood and, in the middle of the night, committed suicide by running out onto the Eisenhower Expressway in front of an oncoming car.

The police unit under Sgt. Groth was divided into two teams—one to come in the front and the other through the back. The Panthers had assigned Mark Clark guard duty. When the police knocked on the door, Mark asked who was there. The police answered, "Tommy." When Mark asked,

"Tommy who?" the police answered, "Tommy gun," and began firing. Mark was hit by a bullet that pierced his heart. When he was falling, his finger pressed the trigger and fired a shot into the ceiling—the only shot that the Panthers fired. The police continued to fire machine gun rounds—both at the Panthers in the living room and at the back bedroom, where they knew Fred would be sleeping. Doc Satchel, Blair Anderson, Verlina Bremer, and Brenda Harris were all shot multiple times. The police intent, as their actions made clear, was to take out the Panther leadership. Brenda Johnson, over eight months pregnant with Fred's child, tried to protect him when he didn't wake up by lying on top of him. Harold Bell and Louis Truelock had not been wounded and ran to the back bedroom to ask Fred what they should do. When the police finally entered after firing ninety to a hundred rounds, they hauled the three Panthers into the kitchen area. Two police went back into the bedroom where Fred was still in bed and put two pistol rounds in Fred's head from above, execution-style. Louis Truelock heard a policeman say, "Bobby is next."

The police left without sealing off Fred's apartment as a crime scene. They even took off the back door and used it like a stretcher to carry out Fred's body—the trophy that had made the raid a success. Black Panther Party members, joined by various support groups, secured the site as the Film Group and the People's Law Office began documenting the evidence. Community members walked by and wanted to see the apartment. The Panthers began conducting tours and realized that the crime scene spoke for itself—all the bullets going one way, toward Fred's bedroom, and no return fire, only a mattress stained with Fred's blood. There was a reason that Rahm Emanuel couldn't allow the Lequan McDonald tape to be released in 2014 before his re-election. Fred's deathbed had an even more powerful effect. When people toured the apartment, they became enraged, horrified, and sickened as the truth of Fred's assassination was plain to see. Cook County States Attorney Ed Hanrahan staged his own version of a "shoot-out" between the Panthers and his brave policemen, complete with a mock-up of the apartment and the officers re-enacting their roles. It was on all the TV stations, and the newspapers parroted Hanrahan's view in their reporting. The black community, however, continued to tour Fred's apartment, and community leaders began to speak out about Hanrahan's lies. Finally, television and newspaper reporters visited the apartment and told their readers that either the Panthers owned guns that shot bullets that magically evaporated along with their shell casings or the police were lying. On March 8, 1970, a People's Inquest was held in a Near West Side church. Six community leaders acted as a jury and found the Panthers to be innocent. Ed Hanrahan was the guilty party.

The Justice Department proposed to handle the brewing legal case involving Hanrahan's raiders and the seven Black Panther survivors by impanelling a federal grand jury in December 1969. Jarvis Leonard convened it. Jay Miller, the Chicago head of the ACLU, warned the People's Law Office lawyers who were representing the survivors that it was Leonard who had personally added Bobby Seale's name to the

Chicago Conspiracy Trial. Leonard promptly presented an indictment of the survivors after a couple of days of police testimony. Judge Epton began their trial on February 11, 1970, and the police testified in a criminal proceeding about the "shoot-out." Less than three months later, on May 8, 1970, Epton dropped all charges against the survivors. The People's Law Office and the survivors were completely surprised. More than five years would pass before Jeffrey Haas would find out the reason for their good luck.

FBI memos that were made available to the People's Law Office through their discovery motions in a related case contained one memo that was dated April 8, 1970. It summarized a deal that was made between the FBI and Ed Hanrahan. The memo was entitled "Victims Summary Punishment," which is FBI speak for "the police meted out their brand of justice on the spot." The Special Agent in Charge of the FBI Chicago office, Marlin Johnson, informed the head of the FBI, J. Edgar Hoover, that Jerris Leonard had assured him the Chicago policemen in Hanrahan's task force would not be indicted, and that in return, Hanrahan would dismiss the indictments against the Panthers within a month. The charges were dropped on May 8th, exactly a month after Johnson sent the memo. Coming a little more than a year and a half after the assassination of Dr. Martin Luther King, Jr., the murder of Fred Hampton would have continued to alienate the Black community and black politicians if this farcical trial had been prolonged. Leonard held up his end of the bargain by calling the seven Panthers to testify before the grand jury early the following week. He then refused to issue an indictment of the Chicago police, though he did present a lengthy report. Far from calming the political discord between Mayor Daley's machine and the black leaders who were allied with him, the lack of indictment provoked outright rebellion by Ralph Metcalfe and a tacit opposition by many others.

When the public pressure did not abate and black aldermen and Cook County Board members demanded some kind of action, a local grand jury was convened in December 1970. Barnabas Sears served as the special prosecutor, and he began to assemble a case against the fourteen policemen. The Chief Judge, Joseph Power, ordered deliberations be stopped in May 1971 so that Ed Hanrahan could present the jury with the police's side of the story. When an indictment was issued in June, Power ordered that it be sealed, cut off Sears's funding, and began an investigation of him. In August the Illinois Supreme Court ordered that the indictment be unsealed. The trial of Hanrahan began on July 10, 1972, with Judge Romiti, who had been appointed by Judge Power, presiding. Since Ed Hanrahan was running for re-election, he wanted the trial over before Election Day. He was found to be "not guilty" on November 1, 1972, but he did not win election as he expected. The Republican candidate for State's Attorney, Bernard Carey, won in heavily Democratic Cook County. The slogan, "Dump the Butcher," produced a large turnout in the black wards of Chicago. The Black Panther Party and other progressive groups helped to get out the vote, and Hanrahan was soundly defeated. Daley's choice as his successor never won another race. In May of 1970, the People's Law Office filed a civil suit, "Hampton v. Hanrahan," for the seven survivors and the two families whose sons were slain. In the fall, the case was assigned to Judge Perry, but the trial did not begin until 1971. Judge Perry was quite similar to his close friend, the infamous Judge Julius Hoffman. It was not surprising, therefore, that Perry dismissed the case on February 3, 1972. Democratic judges have to follow the direction of their political boss, as do Republican judges their boss. A Democratic judge found Fred Hampton guilty of stealing some ice cream bars to pass out to children, and another one found Hanrahan innocent and free from any damages that might be owed the survivors. Such is the epitome of injustice in the judicial system of Cook County, Illinois.

Since an appeal of Perry's ruling would take over a year, the reversal of Perry's ruling didn't occur until 1973. By that time, the People's Law Office (PLO) had begun to receive documents that an anti-war group had made public after raiding an FBI office in Pennsylvania in 1971. Those documents included "COINTELPRO," the counter-intelligence program that was the basis for the police attacks on the Panthers and Fred's assassination. J. Edgar Hoover had been working on such projects since entering the Justice Department in 1917. Serving in the War Emergency Division, he was responsible for arresting Germans who may have posed a threat to America and whose civil rights could be disregarded. By 1919 he led the Radical Division, as it was called, which treated Communists in a similar fashion. By 1924 he was in charge of the whole agency, which was then called the Intelligence Bureau. In 1935 he got its name changed to the Federal Bureau of Investigation. By 1956 he was ready to codify his "dirty tricks" and have other groups assist the FBI. Such tricks included infiltration of informants, burglaries (like Watergate), illegal wire taps, planting forged documents, spreading false rumors, inciting violence through agent provocateurs, and even arranging murders. Since the FBI had been Hoover's fiefdom for forty-eight years, no politician felt safe enough to cross him, not even Presidents.

The Special Agent in Charge of the Chicago Bureau, Marlin Johnson, had already twice attempted to murder Fred Hampton. The FBI tip in January 1969 that got Fred placed in the back seat of the squad car where a gun just happened to be resting and the letter that SAC Johnson himself had written in May 1969 that warned Jeff Fort that Fred wanted to kill him were both failures. Marlin Johnson did lead the raid on the Panther headquarters on July 31, 1969 that made use of a paid informant, George Sams, who had been sent to their headquarters as the excuse for the raid two days prior. The FBI search for a "wanted fugitive" covered up their theft of membership lists and money and the destruction of furniture and the walls. Mayor Richard J. Daley chose Marlin Johnson to become the head of the Chicago Police Board that hears compliments about the behavior of police. The Cook County State's Attorney, Ed Hanrahan, worked with Johnson to implement COINTELPRO through Hanrahan's top assistant, Richard Jalovec. When Fred Hampton appeared on the Key Agitators list of the FBI in 1967, Hanrahan soon charged Fred with mob action. Later he charged him with the theft of seventy-one ice cream bars, and in 1969, he got a conviction. By the end of 1969 he approved the use of the fourteen-man police task force attached to his Special Prosecution Unit to assassinate a leader of the Black Panther Party and member of the Party's Central Committee. Daley's handpicked successor to the office of mayor could not win re-election in 1972. It is important to note that when the civil trial finally ended and the victims received almost two million dollars in damages in 1983, Ed Hanrahan blamed the FBI for its coverup of the lead role that it had played in Hampton's assassination and its willingness to shift the blame onto his shoulders.

The retrial of "Hampton v. Hanrahan," which had been successful on appeal, did not actually begin until January 1976. By then the Church committee had held hearings on Hoover's COINTELPRO and had declared it illegal and unconstitutional. James Montgomery, who was Deborah Johnson's attorney, spoke to Judge Perry about the need to allow the plaintiffs to question the defendants about COINTELPRO and to see the FBI files about their connection to this program. Suddenly, Perry saw the light, and within a week enough FBI files were wheeled into court that would fill twenty feet of shelf space. The PLO lawyers spent most of the summer reading the files and matching the police testimony to memos of what actually occurred during the year of 1969. One of the PLO lawyers, Flint Taylor, later discovered that the FBI had had two agents living above his apartment during the whole time he was in court. They sent a constant stream of reports on all of his activities. Needless to say, the FBI files delivered to the courtroom showed that Fred Hampton was under total surveillance. Judge Perry hoped to get the case dismissed by stacking the jury with law-and-order white jurors and one token black woman. The "hung" jury that led to dismissal on June 28, 1977, could not prevent the case being sent to an appeals court. This time the appeals court could study the FBI documents having been entered as evidence and the defendants' own testimony about COINTELPRO.

Judge Swygert wrote the opinion for the three-judge panel that met with the lawyers for the two parties on August 18, 1978. He basically rejected the Justice Department's argument that FBI defendants were immune because they were carrying out national policy and "acting under orders." Swygert understood the conspiracy and how the Federal Grand Jury was used to cover-up the FBI's involvement. In effect, the evidence already introduced was sufficient to expose the state-sponsored assassination of Fred Hampton. The trial that began in 1979 was different than the two earlier attempts to bring out the truth. Nixon had resigned in disgrace, John Mitchell was out of favor, and the FBI had to act "shocked" that Hoover could have ordered such an assassination. It is understandable, in retrospect, why Hoover took personal charge of the investigation into John Fitzgerald Kennedy's murder and concluded that there was no conspiracy.

Making the goals of the counter-intelligent program of the FBI available to the public meant that the truth of the police state was finally visible to anyone who wished to see it. Mandela gained the same insight in South Africa at about the same time that Hoover was codifying COINTELPRO and unleashing dirty tricks on Civil Rights leaders. The second goal of COINTELPRO—to prevent the rise of a messiah—made it abundantly clear who and what Hoover was talking about: "Malcolm might have been one: instead he is the martyr of the movement." A new documentary on Malcolm X showed that nine FBI informants attended his February 21st speech at the Audubon Ballroom, where he was murdered. His own bodyguard was an undercover New York policeman, just like William O'Neal, Fred's former bodyguard who became the BPP chief of security, was an FBI informant. Malcolm possessed the very quality that Hoover most feared in a black leader—charisma. The dangers of Dr. King, Elijah Muhammad, and Stokely Carmichael in the 1967 version of COINTELPRO that Marlin Johnson had access to were mentioned by Hoover as aspiring to the position of the black Messiah. The third goal of Hoover's program was to pinpoint the troublemakers and put them on the Key Agitators list. Then the FBI could "neutralize" them. Hoover did not specify the means that the FBI would employ, but the examples of Malcolm and Fred show that both the Nation of Islam and the Chicago Police Department could provide willing assassins. Strangely, the FBI's attempt to use Jeff Fort was rebuffed.

Hoover's examples of dangerous black leaders in 1967 contained two red herrings. By grouping Dr. King with the ultra black-racist, Elijah Muhammad, and the opportunist, Stokely Carmichael, should probably be viewed in the light of the fourth goal: discredit black leaders and their organizations.

Hoover's view that Dr. King might turn violent and give up his obedience to "white, liberal doctrine (nonviolence)" showed no grasp at all of what Gandhi's work in gaining India's independence had meant to Dr. King. The high purpose of the Poor Peoples' Campaign—its multi-racial, multi-ethnic attempt to bring the necessities of life to the down-trodden and impoverished, the poor and oppressed people of America is not the first step in bringing the Mau Mau to this land. Hoover not knowing the difference between the lynching and fire-bombing by white supremists and the peace and brotherhood of the Blessed Community might explain why he would neutralize the Nobel Peace prize winner and then take a personal interest in shielding a Ku Klux Klan member from indictment in a bombing.

One question that Fred Hampton's assassination raises is why J. Edgar Hoover thought that it was necessary to kill a man who was so young, who had turned twenty-one just three months prior to his death. Dr. King and El-Hajj Malik El-Shabazz were both thirty-nine and were in the process of forming coalitions that could have threatened the racist, fascist state that Hoover wanted to keep hidden. The FBI director would seemingly have had the same fear about Chairman Fred. His view would thus agree with the views that Elaine Brown and Bobby Rush expressed in court—that Fred Hampton was on the same level as Dr. King and Malcolm X despite his youth. Others who knew Fred well—his doctor, Quentin Young, and the community organizer, Walter Coleman—even believed that Fred Hampton was more advanced than either Dr. King or Malcolm X.

The research presented thus far can perhaps help to answer the question of Hoover's fear of a twenty-one-year-old. Chapters 4 through 6 of this book characterize the activity of the mystery stream of Parzival in the twentieth century. Mahatma Gandhi, Dr. Martin Luther King, Jr., and Nelson Mandela were discussed in the light of the three important leaders of this mystery stream—Parzival, Sir Gawain, and Feirefiz. Malcolm X and Huey Newton were then discussed in relation to their possible connection to Baruch Ahkarin and Gahmuret, two other characters in *Parzival* who possess a stature similar to that of the three main characters. If Fred Hampton were as spiritually advanced as his supporters suggest, then he too would have been a member of the Parzival mystery stream. A fuller discussion of this stream is presented by Bernard Lievegoed in *The Battle for the Soul*. Fred Hampton could not have been the reincarnation of Sir Gawain (Dr. King), Feirefiz (Nelson Mandela), Baruch Alkarin (Malcolm X), or Gahmuret (Huey Newton) since Fred was their contemporary for most or all of his present life. Only Gandhi had already died when Fred was born on August 30, 1948. The other four were alive, and two of them outlived him. The two who didn't outlive Fred (Malcolm X and Dr. King) prepared the way for him to experience martyrdom.

That Fred Hampton is a reincarnation of Mahatma Gandhi is most unlikely. Gandhi died of an assassin's bullet on January 30, 1948. He would have had only two months or so in the spiritual world before returning to the earthly realm to quicken the fetus of his mother, Iberia Hampton, before his birth on August 30, 1948. Iberia had always believed in her son's greatness. She carried the civil case against Ed Hanrahan for thirteen years so that the world might also learn of it. Each year she and her family, along with friends of Fred, attended a memorial service for him at her church and then returned to her home for a sumptuous meal. One reason that such a possible past life of Fred Hampton should not be dismissed out of hand is that Gandhi may have been the reincarnation of Parzival (see chart J). Both Lievegoed and Prokofieff presented research that took the viewpoint that Parzival was one of the twelve Masters of Wisdom and the Harmony of Feelings, who are also called bodhisattvas by the Eastern religions. These great leaders of mankind can be distinguished from us more earthly mortals because of their connection to the world of Providence, which is also called Nirvana in the Eastern world to clarify its difference from the spiritual world, and which is called heaven in the Western world. Since this connection between the human bodhisattva and the world of Providence remains unbroken in the earthly life, the extreme brevity of Gandhi's sojourn in heaven and his sudden reincarnation in Fred Hampton may here find an explanation. When Bernard Lievegoed discussed the past lives of Parzival in *The Battle for the Soul*, he identified Mani as a significant one. He also mentioned that "shortly after the death of Mani, he was apparently on earth again."[18] A similar event that happened to Gandhi may have also occurred to Mani, who was assassinated in 276 B.C. It might also be pertinent to note that Gandhi's biographer,

---

18 Lievegoed, p.89.

Ramachandra Guha, said that "Ever since his release from jail in 1944, Gandhi had spoken often of wanting to live for 125 years."[19] By the time of his last birthday, the battle between Hinduism and Islam for the soul of India so distressed him that he asked, "What is the point of being alive?"

A comparison between Fred Hampton and Mahatma Gandhi could begin with their attitude towards their approaching death. Both men shared a kind of fearlessness that is most rare, as Bobby Rush attested when he spoke at the "Hampton v. Hanrahan" trial. They also shared an interest in the profession of the law. Gandhi studied law and even practiced it briefly in South Africa. For Fred, the desire to become a lawyer had to remain a dream, though both his personal lawyers and his family recall vividly his interest in entering the legal profession. In 1915 Gandhi and his ashram travelled to Shantiniketan. Gandhi was very impressed when he worked in a school where all of the teachers had received nicknames like Mother, Father, Aunt, Uncle and so on. Gandhi believed that having the faculty receive such names inspired a familial spirit to become active in the school. Fred held meetings with the leading members of the Chicago chapter and other important organizers in Chicago. He gave them all nicknames, showing their qualities or characteristics, like "Doc" Satchel and "Slim" Coleman, that are still in use over fifty years later.

One difference between Mahatma Gandhi and Fred Hampton would seem to be their public speaking ability.

---

19 Ramachandra Guha, *Gandhi: the Years that Changed the World, 1914-1948*. New York: Alfred A. Knopf, 2018. p. 82.

Gandhi was so shy in his early life that he could not even read aloud to a group of people a speech that he had written. He was an excellent writer, as his autobiography attests, and he was able to overcome his shyness. His speech to the judge in his trial in 1922 became world historic, and his speeches attempting to heal the split between Hinduism and Islam were equally powerful. Fred developed his speaking ability by listening to tapes of the speeches of Dr. King and Malcolm X. He then practiced mastering the techniques that he found in their speeches. His success in this endeavor is exemplified by his speech in August 1969 after his release from prison—"I Am a Revolutionary." Gandhi is commonly addressed by his friends with the honorific, "Mahatma." The possibility of its truth is generally not entertained, but for a man whose autobiography is entitled *The Story of My Experiments With Truth*, it is actually appropriate. Fred was always referred to by his friends and comrades as "Chairman Fred." The leadership quality implicit in this term, as with Mao Tse-Tung, is also fitting. The chairman of the board is the organizer, and Fred Hampton reflected the planetary influences of Mars even in his body type. This insight into Fred's world-soul-mood leads to the idea that Gandhi's radiant and harmonizing influence may be due to the planetary forces of the sun, and that Parzival's extraordinary shyness may have been connected to the influence of Venus.

A comparison may also be drawn between the death of Fred Hampton and the basic idea of Hoover's COINTELPRO: to prevent the rise of the messiah in the black community, such leaders must be neutralized, i.e., harassed, raided, discredited, infiltrated, and murdered. The crucifixion of Christ Jesus in ancient Palestine involved the treachery of Judas, the deep hatred of the Sanhedrin, and the cooperation of the Roman governor, Pontus Pilate. Willian O'Neal, the chief of security for the Black Panther Party, was an FBI informant who betrayed the trust that Fred had in him. He gave Roy Mitchell the floor plan of Fred's apartment so that the police could focus their fire on his bed and a list of the weapons stored there so that Hanrahan's office could warn off the Alcohol, Tobacco and Firearms agency and other agencies who might take action. The weapons also gave the Cook County State Attorney's office a justification for their four o'clock in the morning raid. Like Judas, William O'Neal committed suicide, though it was twenty-one years later. The deep hatred of many Chicago policemen for the Black Panther Party and Fred Hampton in particular is shown by the photographs that the police themselves shot when they carried Fred's body out of the apartment. Smiles of happiness spread across the faces of the policeman who took part in the parading of Fred's dead body. Many people concluded that this assassination was a Northern lynching. The FBI's director, much like Pontius Pilate, pretended from the beginning that his office had no involvement in Fred's murder. Hoover washed his hands of the crimes Hanrahan committed, as Hanrahan himself bemoaned at the trial's conclusion.

A way in which Fred Hampton's life may be a reflection of events in *Parzival* involves his meeting with Dr. King in

1966. Sir Gawain had saved Parzival from a trance that he had fallen into, and Parzival owed him a great debt. As Walter J. Stein showed in his remarkable commentary on *Parzival*, Parzival began to help Sir Gawain from that time forth, though in hidden ways. The possibility that Dr. King had a life as Sir Gawain makes his devotion to the nonviolence of Gandhi understandable. The meeting of Fred Hampton with Dr. King indicated that the time for Gandhism had past, and that the new form that it would take must answer the needs of all people in this nation, not just black people. Fred Hampton showed its new form in 1969 with the Rainbow Coalition. Dr. King pointed to the same goal with the Poor Peoples Campaign, though his hope to achieve it through an act of Congress would prove to be naive. Actual survival programs needed to be enacted through what Gandhi would have called "self-help." Fred Hampton was able to bring Huey Newton's vision into the Westside of Chicago. But even though he was chosen to serve on the Central Committee of the Black Panther Party, he never actually met Huey Newton who was in prison and was not released until August 1970. The reincarnation of Parzival was not yet able to meet the reincarnated Gahmuret, his father in a past life. The bearer of the family crest of the black panther, Gahmuret, still needed to gain virtue of steadfastness, as symbolized by the anchor of Baruch Alkarin.

When Huey Newton was finally released from prison in August of 1970, the Black Panther Party was in disarray. The attempted merger with the Student Nonviolent Coordinating Committee in 1968 did not bear fruit. James Forman had left to organize in Detroit. Stokely Carmichael and H. Rap Brown may have been firebrands, but they were not organizers. The loss of Fred Hampton, as the FBI correctly surmised, was devastating. Instead of Malcolm's devotion to the people and Dr. King's oratorical ability, the Central Committee came up with a march on Washington, D.C., in a vain attempt to demand a new Constitution based on the ten-point program. When Huey saw the waste of time and resources, he ordered the campaign to cease and party members to return to their cities. He then arranged a trip to China on the basis of his hope to meet with Chairman Mao Tse-tung. Perhaps he felt he could arrange a way to work with one of the most powerful leaders in the world, as he had once served Baruch Alkarin in the ninth century. His hope to gain such support did not bear fruit.

While Huey could not take up the role that Fred would have played, he did write two books—*To Die for the People* and *Revolutionary Suicide*. He also stressed the importance of members and leaders of the Black Panther Party taking up the study of what he called "revolutionary inter-communalism." Huey Newton understood that a dialectical process was at work in the movement from the black nationalism of Elijah Muhammad to the internationalism of the human rights movement that El-Hajj Malik El-Shabazz was trying to develop. Newton believed that a further transformation of that movement could lead to a viable alternative to the reactionary capitalism that international corporations had foisted upon the world.

An important contribution to Huey Newton's idea was made by George Jackson who had been incarcerated most of his life. Like Nelson Mandela, he was an extraordinary organizer and inspired many prisoners to take up their own education and to join the Black Panther Party. Also like Mandela, George Jackson saw through the reforms that the United States government had used to hide the facist state that it had become. Jackson's book, *Soledad Brother*, became an important part of the course of study that accompanied Huey Newton's emphasis on the education of party members. Jackson's article "On Withdrawal," was published in the *Black Panther Party* newspaper in 1971. Coming right after George Jackson's murder by prison guards on August 21, 1971, it explained the idea of the central city commune and how withdrawing from the prevailing culture and developing a proper educational system was a necessary step in freeing the minds of inner city dwellers and building viable institutions to meet their needs. The assassination of George Jackson met all the requirements of COINTELPRO, and having it be carried out by prison guards meant it could be swept under the rug much more easily than Fred Hampton's murder.

By 1972 the various white support groups of the Black Panther Party began to be called Intercommunal Survival Committees (ISC). In Chicago, the People's Information Center was led by Walter "Slim" Coleman. It was next door to the People's Law Office and a close ally of the Young Lords Organization. By joining with other progressive white groups in Wisconsin and Missouri, Slim felt able to take on the task that the leader of the Chicago chapter of the Black Panther Party, Bobby Rush, had asked him to do: organize in Uptown, a poor white community on the North side of Chicago. What had happened to Fesperman and the Young Patriots Organization was not known, but having the ISC move from Lincoln

Park with trained organizers, a cadre, seemed the best way to build community institutions where they were most needed. Uptown was basically a patchwork of migrant groups: Southern whites, whites from Appalachia, Native Americans, Puerto Ricans, African Americans, Japanese, Vietnamese, Mexicans, and Latin Americans. Many of them arrived in Uptown after having been pushed out of other Chicago neighborhoods by urban renewal. They banned together and opposed a plan to gentrify Uptown. Their protests were mostly unsuccessful. When Truman College was built, one thousand two hundred families were displaced.

The urban renewal plan for Uptown had followed the usual scenario. First the housing itself was subdivided into two or more units. Next the landlords stopped making repairs, and city inspectors cooperated by condemning buildings. If "bleeding," as this stage was called, did not suffice to drive out residents, the police were called on to intimidate them. Arsonists were sometimes called on as well. Other methods included building expressways to separate segregated areas from white-only neighborhoods, expanding schools or hospitals (or even building them as with Truman College), and building highrises and luxury stores as gateways to affluent enclaves. The advantage that the Intercommunal Survival Committee had in organizing in Uptown was that many people there had resisted the effort to create a junior college site and many others had experienced urban removal, as they called it, in other parts of Chicago before coming to Uptown. Another advantage came from the extraordinary work that one cadre had carried out in locating the "Chicago 21 Plan" and making a copy of it. This plan for the city of Chicago was basically a blueprint for realtors and developers to gentrify the city by the 21st century and how the city fathers (and the Boss) could assist them. Building strong communities became the key to resisting the masterplan of the developers.

By the end of 1972, an election for Cook County State's Attorney was held, and Ed Hanrahan was running against a Republican, Bernard Carey. The Black Panther Party had never recovered from Fred Hampton's assassination, and it continued to lose members. Bobby Rush did, however, still have many dedicated cadre to sustain the survival programs and to take on the political task of registering black people to vote and to unseat Hanrahan. The tours of 2337 W. Monroe and the Peoples Inquest began the process, but the federal grand jury investigation and the special grand jury and trial which ended on November 1, 1972 kept the issue alive. Mayor Richard J. Daley's goal of grooming his replacement was opposed by the Panthers' slogan, "Dump the Butcher." Daley's machine viewed Hanrahan's job as the key to political power, but they did nothing to repair the fissure that Chairman Fred's murder had caused to emerge between the Boss's black puppet-alderman and the black voters. The shocking election of Bernard Carey opened the way to election reforms and the eventual downfall of machine politics.

The Intercommunal Survival Committee took on the task of forming a multi-racial, multi-ethnic coalition by using what the cadre called community-based organizing (CBO). They sold *The Black Panther* newspapers on street corners as they always had, but they now formed block clubs. They delivered over 600 Panther newspapers to the residents living on those blocks, and they discussed the articles with them. They also listened to them and devised ways to help them. Sometimes the help involved getting stores to stop selling glue to children, who were sniffing it, or getting the city to post speed limit signs and build speed humps on residential streets because eleven children had been killed by speeders. The conversations also led to re-enlivening older organizations like the Black Lung Association, which local residents became active in, and the Park District, which began to provide sports and other activities to children in their neighborhood. Many other programs could be mentioned, but the central idea in all of them was to build a community institution that truly met the people's needs and to encourage community members to take responsibility for it by leading it. People who believe that poor people cannot become leaders have no idea what Gandhi meant by "self-help." The truth is that poor people tend to share and help one another. Instead of using their leadership position to help themselves, they devote themselves to making the institutions help the people they were created to serve.

By 1974 the Intercommunal Survival Committee became the Heart of Uptown coalition. It was a loose combination of the group of organizers and the various block clubs and the community-run organizations that had emerged. A weekly newspaper that focused on the activities of Uptown's progressive, grassroots organizations was published. *Keep Strong* can be compared to Gandhi's *Indian Opinion* in that the Heart of Uptown coalition took collective responsibility for its content and publication just as the Phoenix Settlement had. A service center was also opened to help residents with legal advice and to advocate on behalf of residents experiencing difficulties with city services.

A decision to establish a non-partisan service center was coupled with an effort to prevent Mayor Daley's machine from controlling elections. With the victory over Hanrahan still fresh in mind, a voter-registration campaign was begun. It revealed all too clearly how utterly corrupt Chicago elections actually were. The registration of new voters had become the province of the Democratic precinct captains. Changing that corrupt practice in order to make voter registration accessible and at a convenient time for all residents was a long and painful process. The victory of Bernard Carey and the emergence of groups like Legal Elections in All Precincts (L.E.A.P.) helped greatly. In 1974, Cha Cha Jimenez had returned from living underground and now resided in Uptown. He was asked to become the progressive candidate for alderman of the 46th ward in the election of 1975.[20] Cha Cha's slogan was "Resist the Masterplan," and it helped bring out the vote. He was unsuccessful in his aldermanic bid. Cha Cha and the hundreds of volunteers who worked on his campaign could not win over enough votes in the affluent lakeshore high-rises to win the race. They did, however, send a message to city hall that business as usual was over.

---

20 The strange placement of the Chicago mayoral election between the off-year congressional election of the previous years and the Presidential election the following year was intentional. It was part of the plan of having machine-controlled elections in the city.

With the death of Mayor Daley in December 1976, a power vacuum occurred on the fifth floor of city hall. Michael Bilandic became the new mayor, but the next election in 1979 was no longer a foregone conclusion. By running on a reform platform, Jane Byrne gathered the support of white liberals. She also benefitted from a snowfall that paralyzed the city that works. The Heart of Uptown and other progressive grassroots organizations hoped that she would keep her campaign promise to stop gentrification. She did not, as the organizers, with their ears to the ground, quickly realized. She met with the developers and city-builders, and projects to remove poor people soon emerged. Since the Chicago 21 Plan was still the playbook, Mayor Byrne could not hide the building projects she was approving from the grassroots leaders. They set out to search for a suitable candidate, and they found one. U.S. Representative Harold Washington won the first Congressional district in 1980. He was Metcalf's protégé and now held his mentor's old seat. The Boss of Chicago politics probably disliked Washington even more than he did Metcalfe, whom he hated. On his way up through the Illinois legislature, Washington fought for the very bills that progressive groups supported. He had just navigated the Voting Rights Act of 1965 through the House of Representatives so that its renewal would ensure the protection of voting rights in the South. He answered the request of Slim Coleman and other leaders to run for mayor of Chicago in 1983 by saying that he would run if they could register 50,000 new voters. The four leaders then used the group that they had formed, People Organized for

Welfare and Employment Rights (POWER), to go to thirty-eight public aid and unemployment sites around the city where deputy registrars could register new voters. They continued to register new voters during the regular in-precinct registration period. After two and a half months POWER had registered 250,000 new voters. Harold Washington had to run.

Keep Strong was a transformation of the *Black Panther Party* weekly newspaper but suited to the times and circumstances of Uptown. The *All-City News* emerged as further development of *Keep Strong*, but it included articles on the numerous grassroots groups throughout Chicago and their activities. In 1982 Slim Coleman arranged an All-Chicago City News Dinner with Harold Washington as the keynote speaker. In a room with 150 tables, grassroots organizations from 42 of the 50 wards in Chicago were represented. After Harold spoke, enthusiasm was palpable and the success of the upcoming voter registration drive was assured. Cha Cha also helped the Washington campaign by arranging a rally for Harold in Humboldt Park, which drew a crowd that newspapers estimated at 100,000 people. The idea of a Black-Latino coalition was integral to Washington's vision of a new Chicago. Rudy Lozano and Danny Davis emerged as leaders of the coalition, and they arranged a march and rally that rivaled Cha Cha's. Harold Washington envisioned a third component to his progressive coalition, one that would include the liberal white politicians who had opposed Daley and the various white radicals like Slim Coleman and Mike Klonsky who had fought for the rights of poor white people.

The Democratic primary for mayor was held on February 22, 1983. Jane Byrne and Richard M. Daley split the white vote, and Harold Washington won handily. The repercussions of his victory were felt in the civil trial, "Hampton v. Hanrahan." Ever since the voter registration drive of the previous summer, the FBI saw the danger of extending the trial without the support of the corporation counsel of the city of Chicago. With Washington's victory almost assured, they pressed for a settlement in a last-ditch effort to limit the truth of the key role of the FBI in arranging Fred Hampton's execution from getting out. In April 1983, the settlement of almost two million dollars had been paid out and Washington defeated Bernard Epton, the Republican, in the race for Mayor. The Washington campaign knew that they would win despite the doubts expressed by TV and newspaper reporters. The margin of Washington's victory reached ninety percent in the black wards with ninety percent turnout. Simply put, everyone voted, and the Republicans and Daley loyalists were no match for them.

Harold Washington's first term as mayor of Chicago led to some basic changes in how city hall conducted business. Most important to his supporters was how Washington clarified to the developers that the Chicago 21 Plan was no longer in effect. Gentrification would no longer be at the expense of, and cause the removal of, poor people. His campaign slogan was "Neighborhoods First," and Harold Washington fulfilled it by having developers build more lower-class and middle-class homes and apartments than upper class ones. No mayor before him or after him can say that. The grassroots leaders saw that Washington's concern for making proper shelters available to all extended to creating a program for helping homeless people that became a model for other cities to emulate. Other city services were also changed in an attempt to bring them in line with the ideal of renewing neighborhoods. For example, garbage collection was no longer carried out twice a week in affluent neighborhoods and sporadically in others. It became a regular weekly event everywhere. The event that the FBI most feared came to pass when Washington appointed James Montgomery to be in charge of the 170 corporation counsels employed by the city of Chicago. After his victory in the Hanrahan trial, one of the finest Civil Rights lawyers in the country was now the chief of the corporation counsels and in a position to protect the civil rights of all Chicagoans. Apparently, there was not only a new sheriff in town, but a new judge as well.

With his appointment of Rudy Lozano as deputy mayor, Washington clearly indicated his choice of a successor. Rudy Lozano was a union organizer and a staunch advocate of immigrant rights. By taking on this office, he could become familiar with city government and learn how to use it to help workers, the poor, and the disadvantaged. His assassination on June 8, 1983, has never been solved. It was the fourth assassination of a leader of the mystery stream of Parzival. Like the others, a leader was lost who could not be replaced. Rudy Lozano's murder received scant attention by the press, which was fixated on what they called "council wars." The Vrdolyac 29 carried out a concerted effort to sabotage every initiative of

Harold Washington. Much like the Republicans in Congress in 2008 after President Obama's election, they always and unanimously voted against Mayor Washington's bills. The mayor, on the other hand, saw a much bigger problem with the difficulty of filling city jobs with competent, honest, and caring people. He especially found the selfless leaders of the grassroots groups to be the ideal candidates for the jobs he needed to fill. Even as he did so, Harold Washington always insisted, "Please. Don't let me co-opt you."

The re-election of Washington in 1987 ended the opposition of the machine loyalists. With twenty-six aldermanic races having gone for Washington as well, he now controlled city council. Ed Vrdolyak quit the Democratic Party and became a Republican. With the euphoria and enthusiasm of such a victory, Harold Washington's supporters began to imagine how the corruption in the public school system, the park district system, and other realms of city government could now be addressed, and how human, practical solutions be found. Washington's death from a heart-attack on November 25, 1987 caused a great grief to envelop his supporters. It rained for a week. An era had come to an end. The very next day, the machine bribed Washington aldermen and seized power by electing Alderman Eugene Sawyer as acting mayor. Slim Coleman wrote a book, *Fair Share: The Struggle for the Rights of People*, to explain how Washington's vision could have been expanded had he lived. Washington's experiment with truth, however, showed that city government can become a Blessed

Community. Not just SNCC voting drives or SCLC marches or BPP survival programs can become homes for the spirit of brotherhood and sisterhood—the world soul. A city program to help the homeless, if taken up in the spirit of selfless service to others, can become a temporary home for the Spirit of Truth, the Advocate, and a seed for future cities to build upon. Not despair, but hope should shine from this American form of the nonviolent social movements of the twentieth century. Comparing this movement to that of Gandhi's in India and Mandela's in South Africa should also reveal a similarity in how long they lasted, thirty-three years. Charts O, P, and Q attempt to clarify the three stages of the American nonviolent social movement and how the stages are interrelated.

CHART O

The Grail Circle of Civil Rights and Human Rights Activists in America (1954 - 1987)

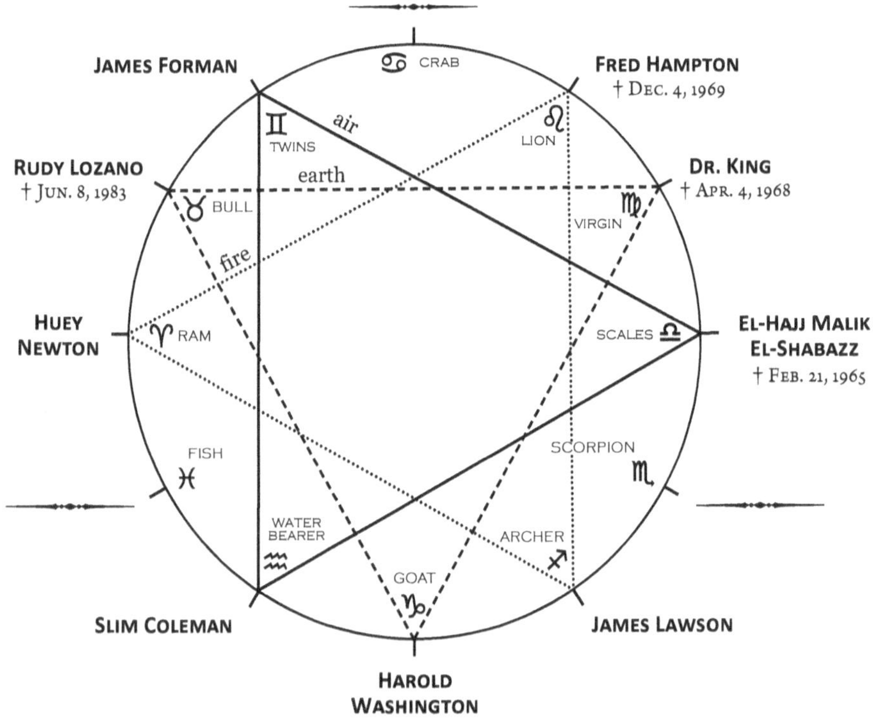

CHART P

The Three Pillars of the Mystery Stream
of Parzival in Twentieth Century America
and the Three Groups of Elements
that Contain Their Co-Workers

ELEMENT OF EARTH (OR WILL)
  Dr. Martin Luther King Jr. (1929—1965)
  Rudy Lozano (1951—1983)
  Harold Washington (1922—1987)

ELEMENT OF AIR (OR SOUL)
  Malcolm X / El-Hajj Malik El-Shabazz (1925—1965)
  James Forman (1928—2005)
  Slim Coleman (1941—   )

ELEMENT OF FIRE (OR SPIRIT)
  Fred Hampton (1948—1969)
  James Lawson (1928—   )
  Huey Newton (1942—1989)

CHART Q

The Civil Rights and Human Rights Movements in America (1954—1987)

        1954—1965   MONTGOMERY BUS BOYCOTT, SCLC,
                              SNCC, MARCH ON WASHINGTON

VIRGO   **DR. KING** — leader of will element
next to   &
LIBRA   **EL-HAJJ MALIK EL-SHABAZZ** — leader of soul element
                    (collaborates with **HUEY NEWTON**)

        1966—1974   BPP, POOR PEOPLES CAMPAIGN,
                              RAINBOW COALITION, ISC

ARIES   **HUEY NEWTON** — collaborator with **MALCOLM X**
in the same   &
fire element as   **FRED HAMPTON** — leader of spirit element
LEO   (collaborates with **SLIM COLEMAN**)

        1975—1987   HEART OF UPTOWN COALITION,
                              WASHINGTON MAYORAL ADMIN.

AQUARIUS   **SLIM COLEMAN** — collaborator with **FRED HAMPTON**
next to   &
CAPRICORN   **HAROLD WASHINGTON** — co-worker of **DR. KING** in the
in the same   element of will
earth element as
TAURUS   **RUDY LOZANO** — third member of will element
                    (goal is to bring selfless service into political realm)

9.
Walter "Slim" Coleman and the Social Movement of Faith and Family Inspired by the Lady of Guadalupe in Twenty-first Century America

In 2016, Slim Coleman decided to publish *Elvira's Faith*, a mostly autobiographical account of his activity in the grassroots struggle for the rights of undocumented Latino families. While he briefly reviewed his activity in the Civil Rights Movement and the Rainbow Coalition, his focus was on what followed Mayor Washington's term as Chicago's mayor. Unlike the death of Fred Hampton which resulted in the slow, gradual weakening of the Black Panther Party, Washington's death caused his coalition to collapse within a single day. Slim pointed out that Washington's supporters had reached an agreement not to criticize those who sold out. Trying to reform the Streets and Sanitation Department, which was notorious for its patronage and Mafia influence, showed Washington's supporters exactly how long and difficult this process would be. It also convinced Slim that politicians had become compromised by arrogance and corruption.

Emma Lozano, Rudy's younger sister, had devoted her life since his assassination to finding out who was behind her brother's murder. After three long years on a fruitless search, in February 1987 she accepted Washington's request to take up Rudy's legacy and run for alderman in the 32nd ward. Since the ward was in the district of the powerful congressman Daniel Rostenkowski, she drew many votes but did not win. Washington then appointed her to the Parent Community Council, which he planned to use to launch his ideas for school reform in his second term as mayor.

The marriage of Slim Coleman and Emma Lozano in 1987 signaled their return to the grassroots organizing that they both believed to be the most honest way to help a community of poor and oppressed people. It also led to the birth of their two daughters. Slim and Emma realized that they would have to improve Kosciusko Elementary School to ensure that their children would receive a good education. One of the new ideas for improving schools that Washington's Parent Community Council recommended was the creation of parent-run Local School Councils for each public school. Emma Lozano was elected president of the Local School Council of Kosciusko, and she set to work on solving the problem of overcrowding.

If the problem of overcrowding in this elementary school is put into the context of House Representative Rostenkowski's control of the 32nd ward, the reason for this problem becomes clear. The Congressman and a group of real estate developers had been "bleeding" the housing that they had invested in so that they would make a huge profit when gentrification began. In chapter two of *Elvira's Faith*, Slim Coleman explained how Rudy Lozano's secret came to their aid. Rudy had discovered the way to defeat the Chicago 21 Plan. When "white flight" occurred, as it had done in this old Polish neighborhood west of the Kennedy Expressway and south of North Avenue, the Latino diaspora coming from Mexico and Central America would fill up the homes that were then available. These hardworking, family-oriented parents could then be organized to resist gentrification if the generation gap between young and old, as well as the split between those parents with "papers" and those who had crossed the Rio Grande and were called "wetbacks" were healed. With Emma's leadership and Slim's grasp of strategy, a unity embracing all Mexicans in the 32nd ward was achieved. Even hired thugs could not dampen their protests. The nightmare that the developers dreaded the most then occurred. Families put down roots, invested in their property, and focused on improving their own children's education.

These Mexican families faced another kind of problem when it came to meeting their religious needs. Most of them were Catholic, but their priest opposed their efforts to provide a better education for their children. He said it was a sin to oppose the government. Tired of his insults, these mothers decided to talk to other priests and ministers to try to find a compatible place of worship. In 1996 they finally decided to form a new church. They named it after a young man who had supported and defended them but who had been killed in a drive-by shooting. Adalberto United Methodist Church combined the eight seasons of faith in the Methodist tradition of John Wesley, honored the Virgin of Guadalupe in the Mexican Catholic tradition, and allowed for a more lively church service with stronger preaching and free flowing prayer in the Evangelical tradition. The difficulty in finding a minister was finally resolved when Slim Coleman acceded to their request to take on that calling. He enrolled in Garrett Evangelical Theological Seminary and received a Master of Divinity degree.

Reverend Coleman's Biblical studies did not cease with his graduation. With each new sermon, he delved deeper into passages in the Old Testament and the New Testament. As an organizer, he had always studied current events and tried to discover their implications and deeper meanings. Now, as a preacher, he combined his two passions, and his sermons began to reveal the various current events in the light of Scripture. When Gandhi had studied the *Bhagavad Gita*, he said that it became for him a dictionary of life. Something similar occurred for Reverend Coleman. He learned to read the events of the day against the backdrop of Judeo-Christian scripture. Another major influence on his sermons came from Liberation theology as practiced by priests in Latin America. He was familiar with the concept of "organizing from below," but the idea of the Latino diaspora and its culmination in the Bolivarian Dream required Reverend Coleman to deepen his research.

Most importantly for the families who attended services was the church's recognition of the Lady of Guadalupe as an active spiritual presence. In 2001 the Roman Catholic Church canonized Juan Diego as the first Native American saint. The pope also declared that the Lady of Guadalupe was the Spirit of the Americas. Her activity on both continents inspired grassroots movements to serve the poor and oppressed Mexicans and Latinos. The depth of Methodist opposition to the worship of this goddess, Guadalupe, was shown when Lincoln United Methodist Church was replanted in Pilsen in July 2009. Methodist ministers actually came to the church in the dead of night with sledgehammers to destroy the statue of the Lady of Guadalupe in a garden beside the church.

When it was time to introduce his book, *Elvira's Faith*, to the public, Reverend Coleman gave a talk on October 26, 2016, at Adalberto United Methodist Church at a book signing event. He said that the activity of the Lady of Guadalupe could be read in the events that revealed her harmonizing and unifying force. Just as the weathercock on the top of a barn shows the direction of the wind, so are certain events signs of her activity. The first sign that Slim pointed to was the defeat of the developers and their plans for gentrification. The unity of Mexican-Americans made this victory possible. Young gang members joined with concerned parents and older Latinos with undocumented immigrants to resist the Chicago 21 Plan and improve Kosciusko Elementary School.

The second sign of the activity of the Lady of Guadalupe began with the partnership forged between Luis Gutierrez, the Congressional representative of the Pilsen-Humboldt Park district, and Sin Fronteras, an organization of mostly undocumented women who in 1997 presented him with thousands of postcards urging him to introduce a new comprehensive legalization bill into Congress. As they began to work together, the Mexican community came to the aid of the Puerto Rican community of

Representative Gutierrez by supporting him against a law partner of Senator Durbin, who wanted a Latino in office whom he could control. This alliance of Mexicans and Puerto Ricans fought for the rights of undocumented families. They formed "the human chain," a mobilization of fifteen thousand people to dramatize the plight of twelve million undocumented immigrants and to pressure the federal government to desist using parts of Puerto Rico as a military firing range.

The third sign of the Lady of Guadalupe showed the broad scope of her activity. Her unifying force had propelled the Mexican families in the 32nd ward to an unlikely victory over the proponents of gentrification. Next she united their cause with the Puerto Rican community in Representative Gutierrez's Congressional district. In 2005 she inspired Father Marco Cardenas to join the Spanish radio host, Rafael "Pistolero" Pulido to protest the slanderous statements of the right-wing paramilitary group, the Minuteman, and their spokesman, Rosana Pulida, about the undocumented community. Father Marco suggested a march that would bring the undocumented out from the shadows and bring home the need for immigration reform. Slim Coleman, Emma Lozano, and Elvira Arellano all helped with logistics, and they encouraged the various other radio hosts who wanted to join in to cooperate with one another. They even convinced Mayor Daley to take part and to speak to the crowd. In March 2005, eight hundred thousand people gathered in Union Park to walk downtown and hear the speakers at the Federal Building. Later that March, Los Angeles held a march for over a million people. Hundreds of thousands marched in cities all around the nation—from Raleigh, North Carolina to Seattle, Washington, to Providence, Rhode Island. The Lady of Guadalupe's reach stretched from one shore of this land to the other. Republicans might oppose her, and Democrats might sell her out, but her goal, as it was with the Untouchable caste in India and with the Black people suffering under Jim Crow or under apartheid in South Africa, was to care for the poor and oppressed. Republicans may label them "illegal aliens," just as Democrats once referred to black people with a pejorative. The truth is that we are all children of God, and we need to become our brothers' and sisters' keeper.

Another sign of the Lady of Guadalupe's presence occurred when Elvira Arellano refused to cooperate with her deportation order in August 2006. She took sanctuary in Adalberto United Methodist Church. In the first six months of her sanctuary, over seven thousand visitors came and signed in to visit and pray with Elvira. In the first three months, Elvira's sanctuary appeared in the media over 20,000 times. Her desire to stay in America for the sake of her son, Saulito, became a national issue, and Elvira became a national voice for undocumented immigrants and for the mixed-status family. The governor, mayor, and many other politicians gave her public letters of support. The U.S. Immigration and Customs Enforcement (ICE) agents could not pay her a surprise visit since they would not be in control of the media coverage. Elvira's sanctuary had become a media event, but the need to present the idea of the unity of the Latino family in a human way required that Elvira come forth and testify in the churches and other public places where she and her son and others in her situation could speak the truth and give a voice to the voiceless. She was not able to do so on her attempted tour in 2007. ICE agents were able to capture here and deport her to Mexico.

The unintended consequence of Elvira's sanctuary was the formation of another alliance. It came about because of a criticism in a newspaper article whose title was, "Blacks Know Rosa Parks and You, Arellano, are no Rosa Parks." Many of Chicago's black leaders knew Slim Coleman and Emma Lozano quite well and had worked with Elvira. Bobby Rush, Jesse Jackson and Louis Farrakhan all rose to her defense, but the accusation itself—that Elvira and the entire grassroots movement were trying to ride on the back of the African American struggle for justice—was not going away. The attack was integral to the Republican Party's plan to prevent a coalition between Black people and Latinos, and it might as well have come from J. Edgar Hoover's COINTELPRO. In an effort to unite the Latino justice movement and the Civil Rights Movement, Luis Gutierrez threw his support to Barack Obama in the Democratic Primary campaign, the only Latino to do so. As part of the Obama coalition in 2008, voter registration drives were held in Latino communities. Protest rallies against mass deportation and mass incarceration (the twin results of President Clinton's Immigration bill and his Crime bill) helped brown and black young people also participate in this new sign of the Lady of Guadalupe's harmonizing influence—the unity of the Movement for the Rights of Undocumented Families and the Civil Rights Movement.

CHAPTER 9   229

The Lady of Guadalupe had worked as the folk spirit of Mexico and of the United States of America, where she was called the Indian princess and the Greek goddess Columbia.[21] In the twentieth century she spread her wings, as it were, and united herself with the nonviolent social movements of Gandhi, King, and Mandela. It was not just in America that Columbia opposed Britannia, the spirit of the British empire, and defeated him, but in India and in South Africa she dealt him two more defeats as well. Just as the Muse had to change to become a folk soul (a spirit of a nation or archangel) so in the twentieth century did she change again and become the Soul of the world. The World-soul then became active in many different nations over a long span of time. She became a spirit of time (a time spirit or an archai.) She was the first principle or leading idea of an era, and the archangels were her messengers. In the present day, the government has been taken over by Uncle Sam, and the Spirit of nonviolence and truth is mocked as impractical. Capitalism controls the political realm, but it is no longer practical. The victories of Gandhi, King, Mandela, Malcolm Little, and Fred Hampton were actually in building organizations that served the community in a thoroughly practical manner with free breakfast programs if necessary. Capitalism and the rule of money cannot lead to a proper form of society; rather community-based organizing leads to people's institutions that actually meet the people's

---

21 See *A Sanctuary for the Rights of Mankind*. See also Walt Whitman's poem "Song of the Exposition," where Whitman suggests that in the Greco-Roman age and in medieval times she was called Calliope, the muse of epic poetry.

needs. The reason that Malcolm Little, Martin Luther King, Jr., and Fred Hampton were assassinated was that the inspiring power of the Spirit of Truth, the Advocate, shown through them. They enabled this spirit to enter into the community and inspire the poor and oppressed to begin building their own new communities, Blessed Communities.

The problem that the Movement for the Rights of Undocumented Families experienced with the Obama administration all came from the same source. President Obama decided that passing the Affordable Care Act was his number one priority and that immigrant reform would be put off until 2011, which essentially meant never since, in the off-year election of 2010, the Republican party swept into control of the House and resumed its firm blockade of immigration reform. The very progressive liberal who had won in 2008 now became the opponent of a grassroots movement, just like President Kennedy had become for the Civil Rights Movement. The March on Washington led by Dr. King in 1963 was originally conceived as a protest march against Kennedy and his failure to pass the Civil Rights Act. A comparison was made previously between the Civil War and Dr. King's social movement. Their similarity is due to the fact that the same spiritual being inspired Lincoln and the Union soldiers at Gettysburg and Dr. King and the Civil Rights activists in the March on Washington. The difference is due to the advance that Columbia had achieved in becoming the Spirit of Nonviolence. In the present age, the class of angels that rules over nations must learn the secrets of the Grail just as mankind itself did a thousand years ago. The Blessed Communities are a

CHAPTER 9   231

reminder, as it were, of the actual goal of the present age so that it may become what the Bible calls "Philadelphia," the city of Brotherly Love.

What President Obama could do to protect and help the Immigrant Rights Movement did not come from a legislative victory, but from his use of executive orders. The modern counterpart of the Battle of Gettysburg and the March on Washington were the executive orders called DACA in 2012 and the further group of executive orders issued before the midterm elections in 2014. Not a great battle or a huge march, but a tour of Familia Latina Unida to the grassroots leaders of the immigration movement throughout the country gave the Spirit of Truth the occasion to speak through children and their parents, giving voice to their love of family and willingness to organize.

What followed the Presidential election in November 2016 could properly be called a reign of hate. An event in the Civil Rights era that would be comparable to it would be the FBI attack on the Black Panther Party in 1969. In the Civil War era, a similar event could be found in the appearance of the Ku Klux Klan following the surrender of the Confederate Army. How President Trump exploited the immigration issue began with the announcement of his candidacy for President. It continued in his campaign with the constant mention of the wall that he would build. It became a nightmare with his use of family separation and torture in the detention centers on the southern border when he took office. The purpose of his demonization of Latinos does have a precedent. Unfortunately, it is not an event most people are aware of or understand.

The successor to President Trump's reign of hate can perhaps shed some light on the actual precedent of Trump's attack on the Latino movement for the rights of undocumented families. By the end of 2019, the coronavirus pandemic had emerged in Wuhan, China and began to spread across the globe. By June of 2020, over a hundred thousand Americans had died. A reign of fear began as people practiced "social distancing," wore masks, and stayed at home. The lack of a vaccine, the increase in unemployment, and the collapse of the economy added confusion to the enforced loneliness needed to mitigate the viral threat that overwhelmed the American health care system. The precedent for this pandemic of the coronavirus (Covid-19) occurred a century ago when the Spanish flu swept over the world, killing fifty million people, more than had died in all of World War I. Admittedly, most people did not observe it at the time, but World War I essentially had the task of stirring up nationalist hatred so that the world economy that was arising at the beginning of the twentieth century could be done away with. Rudolf Steiner, who observed this fact, explained how the world economy brought the competition deemed essential for capitalist economy to an end.[22] With the production of specific goods interwoven among many countries and its distribution also interwoven, the search for new markets had come to an end. President Trump's tariff wars, his opposition to international groups from the United Nations and NATO to the World

---

22 See Rudolf Steiner, *The Karma of Untruthfulness*. Forest Row, Great Britain: Rudolf Steiner Press, 1988. See also Rudolf Steiner, *World Economy*, Rudolf Steiner Press, 1972.

Health Organization, and his friendliness to dictators and war lords may seem to make no sense. His goal was not peaceful coexistence.[23] He foresaw America becoming the greatest (in the sense of most powerful) country in the world and ruling over the lesser nations in a chaotic world where black markets, drugs, and prostitution flourish. No need to fear climate change when nuclear blackmail is a joker in the stacked deck of the gambling houses that President Trump envisions that nations will become.

By signaling a return to national economics, Donald Trump expected the largest and strongest American company to take the lead and push the American economy into a dominant position. In the nineteenth century, that company was Standard Oil. President Trump expected it to return to its preeminent position. His withdrawal from the Paris accords was part and parcel of a belief in American oil companies being able to hold other countries hostage if they are to meet their energy needs. Local communities, however, are not in the same position as state and national governments or the courts or the military. Latinos in general and Latino immigrants in particular have suffered under Trump's national campaign of hate, but the diaspora communities that they are part of are spread across the United States and in every state of the country. The Bolivarian dream is coming into being in the North, and these communities contain the seeds that can transform capitalism into its proper form.

---

23 President Trump withdrew U.S. troops from war zones so that other countries could fight it out to determine which war lord should rule.

Community-based organizing enables peoples' institutions to arise. Not from the top down, but by organizing from below can the seeds be created that will answer the crying needs of the present day. Capitalism, when allowed to run rampant, corrupts government and turns the cultural realm into sporting events and cartoon entertainment. Its opposite, socialism, leads to the bureaucracies of machine politics and economic stagnation. A synthesis of capitalism and socialism is necessary for a humane and free society to emerge. Rudolf Steiner understood how this synthesis could occur, but he believed that it would require a majority of mankind to understand and approve of such a transformation for it to happen.[24] Following World War I, most people were swept up in nationalism and Nazism or bought off by capitalism. They refused to entertain his idea of a threefold society. The ideas of the Village Industries Association (Gandhi), the survival programs (Hampton), and the civics in South Africa (Mayekiso) showed that such seeds can transform local communities. They differ from businesses that seek profits and government programs that provide jobs, since they try to serve the people selflessly by finding ways to meet their needs. Businesses in the future must be run in such a manner. The cut-throat corporate leader must become an anachronism. Businesses serving the needs of the people require that the production of goods, their circulation, and their consumption must be guided and regulated. Only free people with insight into these fields of economic

---

24 Rudolf Steiner, *The Threefold Social Order*. New York: Anthroposophic Press, 1966.

endeavor and possessing a developed sense for the welfare of all can provide such guidance. Joined together in the spirit of brotherhood within economic associations, these people can regulate a capitalist economy properly.

The question of the ownership of capital must be addressed if the full force of Steiner's proposal is to be experienced. Private ownership of businesses in capitalism and public ownership of them in socialism can lead to an insight into their synthesis. The idea of society three-folded into an economic realm, a social-political realm (or sphere of human rights), and a cultural realm, can provide a proper answer to the question of the ownership of capital. Private and governmental ownership of businesses needs to give way to their control by a cultural organization or administration. It would be the cultural administration's role to find astute business leaders to run each company in cooperation with its workers for the sake of society as a whole. When such a leader wanted to step down, the company would revert back to the cultural sphere so that a new leader could be found. No community-based organization would be passed on to a family and be inherited. The proving ground for the necessary changes to the country ruled by Uncle Sam, the Spirit of Capitalism, needs to come forth from the oppressed communities under the care of the Lady of Guadalupe. The body of the world built by capitalism needs the World soul to unite with it in order to become humanized.

www.ingramcontent.com/pod-product-compliance
Lightning Source LLC
Chambersburg PA
CBHW031413290426
44110CB00011B/361